Praise for
Seeing God as a Perfect Father

"When I first became a Christian, I had a lot to learn. Truth is, I still do. Thankfully, God has been patient with me through the years and shown me what it's really like to be His child. But here's the thing: He wants you to discover that same truth in your own life. And I firmly believe *Seeing God as a Perfect Father* is a great place to start."

Dave Ramsey
Bestselling author and nationally
syndicated radio show host

"Olympic gold medals, WNBA titles, and undefeated seasons could easily be described as the most important part of my identity. But it's not! Knowing that I am a beloved daughter of a perfect Father literally changed my life years ago and it's what I count on every day as a professional athlete. Louie's *Seeing God as a Perfect Father* connects with each one of us as he so clearly points us back to our perfect Father. Open your heart and dive into *Seeing God as a Perfect Father* . . . you won't be the same!"

Maya Moore
Four-time WNBA champion, two-time
Olympic gold medalist, WNBA All-
Star and all-time leading scorer

"Some communicators speak to the heart. Others speak to the head. A choice few are able to speak to both. My friend Louie Giglio is one of these. He is both pastor and teacher. He certainly has pastored and taught me. His new book *Seeing God as a Perfect Father* addresses a deep need. May God use it to heal and help us all."

Max Lucado
Pastor and *New York Times* bestselling author

"It's been said that what comes to mind when you think of God is the most important thing about you. In *Seeing God as a Perfect Father*, my friend Pastor Louie Giglio brilliantly and beautifully helps us form a freeing, scriptural image of God. Don't put this important and timely resource down."

Crowder
Grammy-nominated artist, musician, and author

"To know the love of our heavenly Father is both liberating and empowering. The message of this book is both timely and timeless. It will help to heal the wounds and fill the deepest longings of a generation."

Christine Caine
Founder, A21 and Propel

"I believe that God will use *Seeing God as a Perfect Father* to heal hurts in your heart you didn't even know you had."

Levi Lusko
Pastor of Fresh Life Church and author

"It's all too easy to under-recognize, under-celebrate, and under-utilize some of the wonderful blessings we have as Christians. The amazing privilege that we get to call God 'Father' is likely toward the top of the list. Louie's brilliant teaching in *Seeing God as a Perfect Father* is therefore such an important one—reminding us who we are as children of God and reorienting us in our relationship with Him. This wonderful book is a celebration of the Father heart of God and of the life-changing identity we have as His sons and daughters. You'll love it!"

Matt Redman
Global worship leader, Grammy-winning songwriter, and author

"If you're looking for freedom from something done to or withheld from you, *Seeing God as a Perfect Father* will set your eyes on the One who redeems every wrong and stands ready to shower you with every blessing."

Roma Downey
Actress, author, and producer

"Having lost my father when I was younger, I know how powerful it is to know that God will be my perfect Father and that I'll never live a day without Him. My heavenly Father filled every void and never missed a ball game, graduation, or birthday. I believe this book, *Seeing God as a Perfect Father*, will bring hope and healing to us all."

Travis Greene
Musician and pastor of Forward City Church

"*Seeing God as a Perfect Father* is a powerful book that offers a revolutionary promise to us all. Louie beautifully describes a God who is for you and not against you, and he invites us to live as a loved son or daughter of the King."

Scott Harrison
New York Times bestselling author of *Thirst: A Story of Redemption, Compassion, and a Mission to Bring Clean Water to the World*

"*Seeing God as a Perfect Father* is a powerful book. An important book. My friend Louie is right—what you believe about God is not only the most important thing about you but is absolutely crucial to how you live. Sadly, one of the most misunderstood roles of God is as our Father. I lost my own dad when I was only nine months old and know what it's like to lack a healthy comprehension of who God is in that respect. But I have also discovered that embracing God as your heavenly Father can transform your life—filling you with the abiding reality that you are loved, wanted, secure, have a significant purpose in this world, and have an unshakable eternal hope. So I am grateful to Louie for writing such a thoughtful and timely book about the fatherhood of God. My prayer is that through Louie's wise and powerful words, your eyes will be opened to the awesome, sacrificial love God has for you so you can comprehend who you are as His beloved child. Because in this truth is healing, freedom, overflowing hope, and all the eternal blessings God has for you."

Dr. Charles Stanley
Pastor emeritus, First Baptist Atlanta,
and founder, In Touch Ministries

Seeing
God as a
Perfect
Father

and seeing <u>you</u> as loved, pursued, and secure

Other Books by Louie Giglio

Don't Give the Enemy a Seat at Your Table

At the Table with Jesus

Winning the War on Worry

Goliath Must Fall

Putting An X Through Anxiety

The Comeback

Never Too Far

Waiting Here for You

I Am Not But I Know I Am

The Air I Breathe

Seeing
God as a

Perfect
Father

and seeing you as loved, pursued, and secure

Louie Giglio

passionpublishing

W PUBLISHING GROUP

AN IMPRINT OF THOMAS NELSON

To my dad, Louie Giglio.
In spite of all the obstacles you had to overcome with
your father, you were a great dad to Gina and me.

To my father-in-law, Milton "Bud" Graves.
A noble man of honor, wisdom, and strength. It's
hard to quantify how much I learned by watching him.

To every dad who's doing all you can to
shower your kids with a father's blessing.

Contents

And "I will be a Father to you, and you
will be my sons and daughters,
says the Lord Almighty."

2 Corinthians 6:18

Can You See It?!

Low in the Southwest sky on a chilly December night in 2020, something truly special was happening. From the third floor of our townhouse, we could see it. Or, more accurately, we could see *them*.

The orbits of Jupiter and Saturn had positioned the two planets in such a way that they were only one-tenth of a degree apart in the sky, so close as to appear as one to the naked eye. As the sun set, the great conjunction of Jupiter and Saturn lit up the night as if they were one mega-bright star.

What we were witnessing was awe-inspiring. And rare. Though this heavenly coming together of Jupiter and Saturn occurs every twenty years, the last time these two planets appeared this close together was in 1623. Sadly, according to astronomers, due to their position in the sky relative to the sun, the 1623 great conjunction wasn't visible on earth. You would have to go all the way back to March 4, 1226, to find the last time humans were able to witness a similar event.

Seriously?!

Eight centuries had passed since mankind had witnessed such magnificence. Jupiter and Saturn were in rare form. And we were in rare company!

But you might be thinking, *What does the great conjunction of Jupiter and Saturn have to do with seeing God as a perfect Father?*

I'm glad you asked.

In the same way these two heavenly bodies collided in our view that night, providing one stunning revelation, two life-altering truths are colliding in the pages of this book to bring you an eternity-shifting understanding of God.

The first life-altering truth that will come into view is this: *God wants you to know who He is.*

God is not obscure, mysteriously engaging in a cosmic game of hide-and-seek. No, God is announcing His presence with every sunrise and declaring His beauty with every sunset that follows. He has gone the extra mile to pursue you and reveal Himself to you. God wants you to see Him in all His glory and splendor.

The second life-altering truth in these pages is this: *You, like all humanity, are on a desperate search to know who God is.*

Created by Him and for Him, we all have a homing mechanism woven into our existence that propels us toward something more—Someone more. I know that's a bold generalization, a broad-stroke characterization that may have some of you rolling your eyes already and thinking, *Who does this guy think he is? How does he know what I'm searching for? How does he even know what I think about God?*

In making such a blanket statement, I am relying on my expertise in being human. I know what it is to seek the things of this world and yet not be satisfied. I have discovered that under my human longings is a desire to find the One who made me, the God who stamped His very image onto my soul. If this is true of me, it's likely true of you too.

French mathematician and physicist Blaise Pascal famously said it this way: "There is a God-shaped vacuum in the heart of each [person] which cannot be satisfied by any created thing."[1]

Have you felt that tug? Have you sensed a deeper, inner longing for something more?

Pascal concludes that this longing can be filled "only by God the Creator, made known through Jesus Christ."[2]

How stunning would it be if you experienced your own great conjunction as you journey through this book—a beautiful collision of God's desire to be known by you and your desire to know Him. Suddenly, in one glorious revelation, you can find what you've been searching for all along and discover the God who longs to be found by you.

As great as that sounds, there's something more specific that God wants to reveal to you about who He is. God wants you to come to know Him as a perfect Father.

True, God is all-powerful, King, Creator, holy, all-knowing, Ruler, and Lord. But all of God's attributes and names are wrapped in the skin of a Father. A Father who gave you life, made you uniquely you, adores you, and wants to be a part of your life.

At first glance the reality that God wants you to relate to Him in this way can be good or not-so-good news, depending on what thoughts flood your mind and emotions fill your heart when you hear the word *father*. For some the notion of *father* makes you feel secure and strong, loved and led. Yet for others *father* hits differently and surfaces feelings of loss, frustration, and pain. If you find yourself in the latter camp, hearing that God wants you to know Him as a Father can be a struggle.

Sadly, it's not a secret that many children are born into homes without a dad present. Add to this reality divorce, death, distance, dysfunction, and disinterest and there are a lot of us left to wonder if we matter to our earthly father at all.

I've been sharing the *Seeing God as a Perfect Father* message for decades. I've seen how this message can land differently in people's hearts and minds. Years ago after speaking to a group of college students, a young man told me, "If God is like my dad, I'm not interested." Fortunately, God is far better than any earthly father, especially the one who left a broken relationship and a broken heart in his wake.

Here's the good news: God is not a bigger version of your dad. He's the perfect version of your dad—and more. That's the hopeful beauty in the great conjunction God is waiting for you to discover.

In one incredible collision we find that we can live with the Father's blessing in our lives and walk in an intimate relationship with the God of creation. We can know God as a Father who is perfect in all His ways. What's more, we can come to know who we truly are in Him—loved sons and daughters of a perfect heavenly Father. He can transform our lives through the power of that perfect love so that no matter what loss we have endured in life, we can live free.

Whether we think about that potentially painful experience or the happy experience of knowing the embrace of our earthly dad, most of us would admit we really want and need the blessing of a father. We want to hear our dad say, "I love you. I'm proud of you. I'm here for you."

This is precisely why God is revealing Himself as a perfect Father. He wants you to relate to Him in this way. He wants you to live knowing that the God of creation loves you as His child. He wants you to live under the waterfall of His blessing.

God is not a riddle to be solved. He is a revealing God. He wants to be seen. He desires to be known. And God has been seeking you since before you were born. You were made by Him and for Him. That's why you've been searching for something of meaning beyond the here and now.

God's most visible and complete revelation is found in the person of Jesus Christ—God in human flesh. At His birth, when something similar to the great conjunction appeared in the ancient sky to lead the wise men to Him, they called Him Emmanuel, which means *God with us*.

In Christ, God was lighting up the darkness in an unmistakable way.

Can you see it?

On that Monday in December, Shelley and I were fortunate to have a clear shot at Saturn and Jupiter from the third-story landing above our stairs. Just over the building across from us, in a gap between the towering pines, we could see this rare phenomenon with our own eyes. A close-up view through star-gazing binoculars made it even more incredible, but the point is, given the mid-rise condo buildings in our area of town, we were blessed just to have a glimpse at all.

But you don't have to worry whether or not you'll get a good view of what God wants you to see. He's made sure His love for you is visible from anywhere on the planet.

Jesus has made God's love for you profoundly clear. He gave His life for you on the cross so that you could be born again through faith in Him. More specifically, Jesus gave His life for you so that you could become a child of God.

Did you catch that?

Jesus took on your sin and shame and died in your place so that you could become a child of God! So you could know who and whose you are. So that you could call the almighty God your Father. So that you could live with a perfect Father's blessing all the days of your life. So you could grow up and be like Him.

The great conjunction of a new relationship with God awaits us. Let's get started as we turn the page and take a deeper look at this desire for a father's blessing.

Chapter 1

Craving a Father's Love

When I was growing up I always loved anytime my dad showed up for my Little League game or, when I was really young, for an afternoon at the swimming pool.

Our apartment complex had two pools, one of which was close to Building 29, where we lived. That's where you'd find me and my friends on summer days—running, jumping, diving, splashing. But Dad worked during the days, and Saturdays were reserved for golf, so that meant he didn't often make it to our neighborhood pool hangs. But like most kids, I always held out hope that my dad would show up.

By the way, this is no knock on moms. Of course Mom was at the pool. Who else would have carried the floats and the cooler and the towels and snacks?! (Moms, we love you!) Mom was often the underappreciated, stabilizing force in our universe—like gravity or Newton's laws of motion.

But when Dad made an appearance, I'd lose my mind!

Memories like this one take me back to our annual family

vacations in Florida when I was growing up. Our family stayed in the same motel every year, a fairly simple 1960s setup right on the beach, consisting of two double-story buildings, their efficiency rooms facing one another across a grassy lawn. The swimming pool was tucked in between the two buildings near the parking lot.

All of us kids (we normally took our vacation with two or three other families) spent most mornings in the pool waiting for our dads to return from their deep-sea fishing outing or their early morning round of golf. When the dads showed up back at the motel, surely exhausted from being out in the sweltering heat, the oh-so-common exclamation arose from the swimming pool.

"Dad's here! YAAAAAY!"

Our excitement soon led to chants of: "Dad, Dad, come in the pool!" Soon followed by the invariable cry:

"Daddy—watch me!"

As soon as Dad arrived I couldn't wait to show him what I could do, what I had learned—my best dive, my best splash, my best underwater swim, my best jump. So I'd call out again, and I'd call out louder: "Daddy! Watch me! Daddy! Daddy! Look what I can do! Watch me float on my back! Watch me jump into the pool! Watch me, Daddy! I'm going to do my running dive! Hey—look at me! Are you watching me, Daddy? Daaa-aaa-aaa-dddy!"

What was happening in that moment?

Maybe I wanted so desperately for my dad to look my way. I wanted him to validate my new skills. I wanted him to acknowledge how special I was to him. I wanted him to celebrate what I could do. I wanted him to cheer for me.

Maybe I simply wanted him to look my way and say, *I see you.*

I wanted him to *be there.*

For me.

Can you still feel that moment—or a moment just like it?

Maybe for you a scene like this one played out on the trampoline in the backyard. Or maybe it unfolded at your basketball game when you noticed your dad walk into the gym during halftime. Or maybe your "dad's here" moment happened at your piano recital when, after peeking repeatedly around the curtain before your turn to perform, you finally saw the outline of your father's frame in the doorway.

In each case you weren't implying Mom's opinion didn't matter—that her approval wasn't important. In fact, I want to say off the bat that this book is not intended to discount the amazing and irreplaceable role moms play in our lives. Their blessing is essential, and we can't fully flourish in life without it. It's just that there is something different—and special—about what your daddy thinks about you.

That Primal Craving

Maybe that father's blessing has been present in your life. But maybe it hasn't. Maybe the pool episodes described above are far-off dreams for you, something you might have longed for but never experienced. Or maybe the blessing was there for a time, but then you sensed it slipping away. Or maybe the approval was never there in quite the way you wanted it to be. You always felt it was performance-based, not unconditional.

That's the raw spot we want to go to in this book. Because that longing for a father's affection and approval is innate and universal—and a lot of us didn't always get what we were desperate for from the man who was responsible for bringing us into this world.

That longing is unquestionably there when we're growing up. We crave our dad's attention and approval when we're little kids, and we want so badly to hear him say:

"That was incredible, baby girl."

"Wow, Ace (that's what my dad called me), that was the best game of all time."

"I see you, Princess! Do it again!"

"Way to go, son! You're getting so much better!"

Yet that longing is still there when we're older, too, even though it may show up in different and more complex ways. Every one of us is desperate for the approval of a father—no matter what our age. A recent study in *Psychology Today* underscores this need for a father's approval, even at the stages of life where we have matured and reached levels of success. Dr. Peggy Drexler writes:

> In my research into the lives of some 75 high-achieving, clearly independent women, I knew that I would find powerful connection between them and the first men in

their lives. . . . What surprised me was how deep (and surprisingly traditional) the bond is, how powerful it remains throughout their lives, and how resilient it can be—even when a father has caused it grievous harm. . . . No matter how successful their careers, how happy their marriages, or how fulfilling their lives, women told me that their happiness passed through a filter of their fathers' reactions. Many told me that they tried to remove the filter and—much to their surprise—failed. We know that fathers play a key role in the development and choices of their daughters. But even for women whose fathers had been neglectful or abusive, *I found a hunger for approval.* They wanted a warm relationship with men who did not deserve any relationship at all.[3]

Did you catch that key phrase—the "hunger for approval"? The same can be said for sons as well as daughters. According to Dr. Frank Pittman, author of *Man Enough*, "Life for most boys and for many grown men is a frustrating search for the lost father who has not yet offered protection, provision, nurturing, modeling, or, especially, anointment."[4] That word *anointment* refers to being chosen, blessed . . . approved. We are all desperate for our fathers' approval. But it's not always there.

Without this approval, we can feel given up on, abandoned, deserted, or disowned. We can feel ignored or isolated or jilted or judged. There's some kind of thirst we can't quench on our own, a hole we cannot fill no matter how hard we try. This void, this lack of a father's presence and approval, can feel like a shadow that is always there, an intangible missing piece we don't even know how to find. In the words of Dr. Drexler, our happiness or satisfaction or contentment or peace still passes through "a filter of [our father's] reactions."

And when that approval isn't there, we feel like we don't matter. Maybe the word you would have chosen would be *angry*. Or *abandoned*. Or *forgotten*. Or *all alone*.

However you describe it, underneath it all is a sobering sense that your father cared about something else more than he cared about you.

But know this—the God of heaven is not moving on without you. He's not walking out on you or trying to inflict pain on you.

I know that even mentioning this need for a father's approval might be problematic for you, striking a nerve close to the surface or tapping into a hurt you tried to bury eighty feet underground, and you're thinking, *I don't want to go there.* It's also possible that although you're just a few pages into this book, you realize the issues with your dad are more real than you'd like to admit. Maybe the walls are already rising around your heart.

On the other hand, some of you had great fathers, and you know what it's like to live in the rays of a father's blessing, the marvelous light of a father's love. If that's the story of your life's journey, that's something to celebrate and be grateful for, but don't toss this book aside thinking it's not for you. I promise there's a great reward waiting for you in these pages as you discover more of what it means to be a loved son or daughter of the King.

The God of heaven

is not
moving
on
without
you.

The greatest likelihood is that many of you have never known the blessing—or the *full* blessing—of your earthly dad. What's worse, some of you are stuck with the fact that the possibility of ever hearing your dad say, "I love you and I'm proud of you," is gone—washed away by death or distance or disinterest. The blessing you long for is mired in a pit of regret, pain, or abandonment. This is your reality, and there's little or nothing you can do to change it. You feel like it's too late.

All of us have different experiences with our dads. But what unites us is the need that's woven into our souls—the need to be loved, and treasured, and noticed, and accepted by our fathers. No matter how defiantly we may try to dismiss the craving that's in our hearts for a father's blessing, we are all incomplete without it. Deep down we all simply must have it. We all are incomplete without it. Our lives move on from the summer days at the pool as kids, but the need for a father's approval is always there.

I understand that this book is landing in the hands of people from all walks of life and all ages. If you're twenty-three years old and coming off the heels of eight years of misery since your dad split, then you may be more in touch with what I'm saying than others. But it's also true that if you are a forty-nine-year-old living on the Upper East Side of New York City whose career is booming and who is reading this right now at your Hamptons weekend house, you are just as likely to be in desperate need of the approval of your father.

We're all intrinsically wired to flourish under the waterfall of our father's blessing. If something goes wrong and that needed flow is diverted, the sting we feel is real, and the downstream consequences cannot be ignored—even if we try to push them into the distance.

For me this came into super-clear focus when I was eighteen years old and one of the biggest decisions of my life seemingly came out of nowhere. Like a lot of college freshmen, I didn't yet have a solid life map. My plan was to ride the wave of tennis as far as I could. Having made that the main obsession of my life through the later years of high school, I thought I'd give it a go at Georgia State University and hope for the best. Yet that train didn't even get out of the station before I sustained an injury early in fall tryouts. I soon realized this path was both unrealistic (I just wasn't good enough) and unattainable because of the torn muscle in my side, even if I had been good enough. I could have chosen to grind away at it, but I'd be so far behind I'd never catch up.

But God had a different plan anyway.

He hadn't gifted me to crush one-handed backhands with pinpoint precision. No, my skill set orbited in the zone of communication. Public speaking, to be specific. Though I hadn't fully realized it for myself, I was totally at ease speaking in front of people (though researchers say this is the number one fear of most people) and had above-average ability to do so. That led to opportunity, whether speaking to the student body at school or giving a short talk on a mission trip with the youth group from church. And that led to a path I never could have imagined back when I tore that muscle in my side.

Whenever an occasion arose where someone needed to step up and speak into the moment, people invariably looked my way. And while those early attempts at influencing and encouraging people through spoken messages were rough around the edges, people would say I did well, and then more opportunities would come my way.

Shortly after my tennis dream went down the tubes, untangling my heart from that obsession, God arrived with a startling announcement—He was calling me to preach. I'll admit I hadn't seen that one coming, but it made sense. All of my experiences and passions, as well as my budding ability, aligned with His call. It felt like I was suddenly zeroing in on understanding the unique way that God had gifted me and seeing how that might lead to a life path.

Our Intrinsic Wiring

God has wired each of us with unique abilities, aptitudes, and desires. Somewhere amid this lies our created gifting—the pathway that we will follow on earth. The heart of our reason for being is to know and love our Maker and enjoy Him forever. Nothing is more important than that; nothing surpasses that core purpose. Yet within our relationship with God, He tailors us to make our unique contributions to the greater good for His glory, giving our individual lives very specific meaning and direction.

His plan for you is not mere existence. It's way beyond

mere drudgery or a job you can't stand and aren't good at. He has woven into your heart a gift and a dream so that you can invest your days in meaningful pursuits that make your heart come alive and help others' hearts come alive also.

Back at Georgia State with my newfound calling, I began to understand that my purpose was to tell the story of Jesus to the world. This realization was accompanied by trepidation and excitement, but my heart was on fire with a desire to say yes to God, a desire that overwhelmed my fears. My pastor encouraged me to devote two weeks to prayer and to immerse myself in God's Word.

At the end of the two weeks, I had my answer and was ready to tell my church that I was surrendering my life to God's call to ministry—to preach.

I was pumped, except for one thing: I needed to tell my dad.

My dad was awesome. But when it came to the most important part of my life—my relationship with Jesus—we didn't have much common ground. Our family was bi-denominational from the start. Dad was a nonpracticing Catholic and an on-and-off attendee of our Baptist church but was never much of an adopter of the "Jesus way." Mom was a praying saint. She was all in for Jesus and the church. Mom was going to be thrilled at my calling. There was no problem there. But Dad wasn't going to know how to process my decision, and I wasn't sure how I was going to tell him. So I put off talking to him about it for as long as I could.

The days rolled by, and suddenly it was the Sunday

afternoon before the evening service where I planned to announce my decision during the response time at church. I knew time was running out. I couldn't make such a declaration in front of the whole church without telling my dad first. But how could I break news like this to him? Later that afternoon I walked into the kitchen of our apartment where my dad was warming some leftovers on the stove. I swallowed hard, opened my mouth, and heard words coming out.

"Dad, I have some big news. I feel like God is calling me to be a preacher. I'm going to tell the church at the service tonight, and it would be great if you could be there."

Awkward pause.

Dad just blanked. He was shocked. Caught off guard. Granted, I'd put him in a tough spot by springing the news of my decision in such a haphazard way. Finally, he managed to get out the words, "That's great, Ace."

But his expression said it all.

I could sense the wheels turning in his head—*my son is going to be a Baptist preacher.* All of his golf and poker buddies' sons were either playing football for Auburn or planning to be attorneys or accountants or something respectable. One friend's son was going to take over the family business. This week, while a new hand was being dealt at the Friday night card table, the question would eventually come: "Lou, what's your kid doing, again?"

Um, he thinks he's going to be a preacher.

That's the last thing my dad wanted to say through the haze of cigarette smoke around the poker table. God had placed a captivating calling on my life, but as far as I could tell, my dad was disappointed. I knew from that initial moment standing in the kitchen on that Sunday that we might never be able to fully share in the journey I was embarking on for the rest of my life. In the days that followed I could sense a tension building in my heart. On the one hand I was so pumped about finding my true calling in life. But on the other hand I also really wanted my father's approval. I wanted his blessing.

Sadly, my dad didn't turn up at the church service that night. What at first was an awkward gap between my walk with Jesus and his was now a little gash—right in the side of my heart. I knew Dad didn't mean any harm by not coming, but it hurt a little anyway. More than anything, I just wanted to have his approval.

Don't we all? We want our dads to see us. To acknowledge what we can do. To value who we are. To cheer for us and tell us they love us.

I understand that for some of you, the story about my dad's reluctance to initially celebrate my calling will resonate, while for others it produces a completely different range of emotions. You're thinking, *You're lucky, Louie. My dad wasn't even there to talk to about my life choices and big decisions. And if he had been, he just might have knocked me across the kitchen in anger and cursed God.*

Or for some of you, the phrase you heard when you confided in your dad about your dreams was, "Good luck with that. I doubt you'll ever amount to anything."

Maybe your dad mocked your ambition. Or maybe he tried to superimpose on you his plan for your life.

We all have different experiences with our dads, but the craving for our father's approval is the same.

Some of you possess that blessing fully and are thinking, *I love my dad!* When you shared your dreams with him, he gave you that assuring nod and grin and told you he'd do everything he could to help you. That kind of father is a gift, and if you have a dad like this, I hope you'll thank him again today! Yet for others there's a palpable, uneasy silence right now as you're reading, and you're thinking about bailing on this book. You don't want to peel back the layers of your heart to examine your relationship with your dad. It's too painful, and the hurts are too recent, too real.

But I encourage you to stay with me. Keep reading. Why? Because God is offering you a promise that has the power to change your life forever.

The Heavenly Father's Response

The promise is this—no matter where things are with your earthly dad, you have a perfect Father in heaven who loves you and wants to pour out His blessing on you.

The Scripture says it this way: "Even if my father and mother forsake me, the LORD will take me in" (Psalm 27:10 NABRE).

Even if the blessing of our dad escapes us, the love of

our heavenly Father can still find us. Even if our dad is no longer with us, our Father God can still hold us close and lift us up. Just because we have experienced a breakdown in our relationship with our dads, it doesn't mean we can't experience a miracle recovery in our relationship with God. Even though we may bear wounds inflicted by our dads, God can restore us and raise us up healed and whole.

This may be a far-fetched notion for you, like some pie-in-the-sky promise that's impractical or impossible. Or you may be thinking, as a lot of people do, *If God is anything like my earthly father, then I don't want anything to do with Him anyway.*

We all have different father stories to tell. Mine is mostly a good one; and although my dad wasn't perfect, he loved my sister and me and did his best. Your experience with your dad may be the worst, a tale marked by tragedy that's too painful to even talk about. But here is the possibility we will uncover in this book: no matter what has happened on this side of eternity between you and your dad, you are prized and sought after by God.

Maybe you can quickly recount the exact places and times and ways you were left behind by your dad. You were abandoned. The memory is vivid and real. You were knocked down. You were lied to. You were hurt. You were rejected. You were devalued. You were ignored. You were held to a standard that no one could meet.

Yet even when we are forsaken by the one whose blessing we need the most—one of life's most debilitating blows—there is still a staggering promise available: "The LORD will take me in."

God is a Father, but He's not the same as your earthly dad. His heart is good, and His arms are strong.

While your life story to date may be a tangled mess of betrayal, disappointment, and defeat, history records that the God of heaven is for you. He made you. He sees you. And He wants you to know the joy of being a child of God and of having the most excellent Father possible. He Himself wants to be your Father, and He wants to shower you with His blessing. He wants to raise you up, show you the ropes, help you grow strong, and cheer you on as you pursue your God-given passion. He wants to put a safety net of His love under you so you can spread your wings and take flight without the crippling fear of failure holding you down.

It's not the same as having your dad back or having him become a different kind of father than he was or is. But the blessing God wants to give you is not to be discounted. In fact, the blessing of Father God is actually way beyond any human relationship. The best possible earthly father giving the most excellent blessing can't compare to the smile of your heavenly Father. His love is supernatural and powerful, unending and unassailable. And His love means this for us:

No one who knows Him as Father will be left behind.

No one will be orphaned.

No one will go unwanted.

No one's story will end with abuse and betrayal.

No one will have to live without a father's love.

No one, ever.

Taking the Leap

All God is asking you to do is to give Him a chance. As we journey together through these pages, He wants to open your eyes to see Him as the kind of Father He truly is. He wants to tear down any misconceptions that have formed in your mind about Him as a result of your experiences or because of what you've heard others say about Him. And He wants to walk with you through the hard stuff, the pain you have endured as a result of a broken or strained relationship with your dad.

God wants to bring you to the place where you believe and receive that what He says is true when He's talking about you as a son or daughter of the King of the universe. And He wants you to live fearless and free. He always stands poised and ready to take a step toward you. You just need to give Him the nod, then simply be willing to take a baby step toward Him.

Let's go back to that summer day at the pool, because it can help us understand what this step toward God is going to look like. For me, Dad's arrival at the pool uncorked cries of "Daddy, watch me," and sometimes, if I was lucky, Dad would jump into the water with me. That's when things got really fun. It mostly meant trying to "dunk" my dad—to get him underwater by wrapping my arms around his head and putting all my weight on him—something I never managed to do until I was in my teens.

But when I was younger, Dad always wanted me to jump to him from the edge of the pool. Did anyone else experience this? I barely knew how to swim, but Dad wanted me to jump. Standing in waist-deep water a foot or two from the edge of the pool, he held his arms out and beckoned me to "jump!" Unsure, I looked at the water—a seeming ocean waiting to swallow me up—and then back at Dad. Water. Dad. Water. Dad. Mom. Water. Dad.

Eventually, I jumped, overcoming my fear—and discovered that Dad's heart was good and his arms were strong. I'd repeat this as Dad backed farther away from the side of the pool and called me to trust him more. Each time, his heart was good, and his arms were strong.

Maybe for you there was a hiccup in the mix because crazy Uncle Billy got into the action and he was a little devious or deranged and actually backed away as you took flight, allowing you to sink into the abyss before he plucked you to safety. You're still a little scarred by it even now. But by and large most dads were true and trustworthy. Their hearts were good and their arms were strong. The result was a brief moment of airborne terror followed by a lot of laughter and joy once in our fathers' hands.

In the same way God is inviting you to take a step toward Him. It may look risky, and you may be fighting thoughts that cause you to run from the notion, fearing you'll plunge to the bottom of the deep end. If you come up at all, you'll resurface the pain of the past. Or, something may be telling you that if you jump, God will be like crazy Uncle Billy, and He'll let you down.

But here's the more likely scenario: after a small and uneasy moment while you begin to loosen your grip on whatever you're using to cope with the absence of your father's blessing, you'll take that tiny jump, and you'll find your heart laughing in the arms of a Father who is offering you the best blessing you could ever know.

The journey through these pages may not be pain-free, but I am confident in the power of the message in this book and have seen it transform hearts throughout the years. As I mentioned in the prologue, I've been sharing these messages for a long time. I first shared them at a college Bible study more than thirty years ago, and I've had the privilege of sharing them with singles, teens, and people of all ages. Every time I share them, God breaks through in people's hearts (including mine) and opens eyes to see Him like He truly is. I'm praying and believing He's going to do it again—for you.

Knowing God intimately as a perfect Father that you can love and trust and lean on and follow may seem like a mirage in a desert of deflated hopes and dreams. But it's both possible and likely that by the time you finish the last page of this book, you'll be in a completely different place in your approach to God and in your understanding about the way He's been pursuing you all this time.

The groundwork comes next. I invite you to turn the page and keep reading, because it's time to discover the most important thing about you.

Chapter 2

The Most Important Thing About You

The desire for a father's blessing is one of the most powerful forces in our lives. And the whole point of this book is to help you find freedom as you come to experience God as a perfect heavenly Father.

But there's something even more powerful, more essential, more central to who you are that we need to explore together first. It lays the groundwork for our coming to know God in a personal and intimate way, and I'd venture to say it's the most important thing about any person—including you.

- It's not where you're from.
- It's not your level of education.
- It's not what other people think about you.
- It's not even what you think about yourself.
- It's not what kind of family you have.
- It's not what your gifts and abilities are.

- It's not what you've overcome.
- It's not what you own or don't own.
- It's not what you've done or haven't done.
- It's not your personality type.
- It's not your looks, your smarts, your friends, or your clout.
- It's not your wins or your losses.

Nope. The most important thing about you is *what you think about when you think about God.*

That may make total sense to you, or it may come as a bit of a surprise. I know it's a big statement, but if you think about it carefully, you'll see that nothing about you matters more than what you think about God. This is the most essential and defining thing about you.

One of my mentors early in life, Dan DeHaan, painted this idea so vividly for my friends and me when we were teenagers. I can still hear him saying it in one of his talks at our summer camp: "The most important thing about you is what you think about when you think about God." Dan's eyes would light up when he said it. In fact, his eyes would light up any time and every time he started talking about God.

By and *For*

I came to discover a few years later, after his sudden death, that Dan was greatly influenced by another legendary voice from a previous generation: theologian and pastor A. W. Tozer. In his well-known book *The Knowledge of the Holy*, Tozer says it this way: "What comes into our minds when we think about God is the most important thing about us."[5]

Why did Tozer make such a blanket statement about all of us? Why would he write something so all-inclusive, so powerful and comprehensive, about you and me? Did he know us? Did he know anything about your life and your story or mine?

Tozer didn't need to know us individually because he knew what God says about us in Colossians 1:16, where we find the cornerstone of this truth. This Scripture says, "All things were created by him, and for him" (KJV).

Did you catch the dual emphasis in that verse? First, you were made *by* God. He is your source of origin. You didn't make yourself. You didn't happen randomly or by some cosmic accident. Since God made you, you are incredibly important, valuable, and prized. And second, you were made *for* God. That's your central purpose on planet Earth now and into forever. When God made you, He didn't just plunk you down on a rock in space and wave goodbye, never to have anything to do with you again. The reason He made you was so you could connect with Him in a vital relationship. Hardwired into your DNA is a response mechanism that enables you to do exactly that.

Since we were made *by* God and *for* God, our hearts search for the God whom we were made *by* and *for*. Our souls want to respond to Him. Like a homing device, there's something in all of us that draws us magnetically toward God.

"We tend, by a secret law of the soul,

to move toward our mental image of God."

A. W. Tozer

Yet plenty of people fight this draw. They try to ignore the pull. They push the idea of God out of their worldview and try to pretend the draw doesn't exist. But God can't be ignored. Not ultimately. Eventually everybody acquiesces to the draw and at least thinks about God, even if they never admit it out loud. That's because the force that pulls us toward God is built directly into our souls. We were designed to sense this pull within us.

Acts 17:25–28 talks about how God "gives everyone life and breath and everything else," and that He did this so we "would seek him and perhaps reach out for him and find him," for "he is not far from any one of us." That's a repeat of the same idea—that we were made *by* God and *for* God, and because of that, we are constantly drawn toward Him.

If you've ever felt a tug in your heart toward God, that's the hardwiring of the primary response mechanism at work. God placed the tug there. The nuance of the original language in Acts 17 means we grope for Him as if we're in a darkened room with blinded eyes and a cluttered floor, trying to feel our way forward. We know there's something greater than us out there—stronger, bigger, and more important.

The language of Acts 17 doesn't portray God as some sinister being with a twisted sense of humor making us stumble through the night in search of Him. Rather, the picture is of what sin has done to you and me; it has blinded us from seeing the One who fashioned us by and for Himself as we grasp for lesser things that cannot ultimately satisfy the longing in our hearts.

Who are we looking for? Where? Fortunately, Acts 17 says that God is "not far from any one of us." And a little later in *The Knowledge of the Holy*, Tozer added this thought, which goes along with Acts 17: "We tend, by a secret law of the soul, to move toward our mental image of God."[6]

If we are all moving toward our mental images of God, then we certainly need to move toward the right mental image, the accurate idea about God, the true picture. We've established that at some point we all move toward *our concept* of who we think God is. But some of us might be moving toward a faulty or harmful image. Since this image is the most important thing about us—since it forms our identity and provides security and purpose and mission and governs our actions and heart attitudes—it needs to be correct!

What's Your View of God?

If you had a sketchpad in front of you, and I said, "Quick, draw a picture of God," what would you draw? I don't mean a physical picture of skin and limbs and hair but a picture of what God is like in His essence.

Everybody has a picture of God in mind, and there are a ton of different viewpoints—some of them good, some of them not so good. Your concept of God could have come from a lot of places. Maybe your mom and dad told you at a young age what God was like, and you incorporated a lot of their ideas—some helpful, some harmful. Obviously, the religious culture and the part of the world you grew up in played a big part in shaping your image of God.

Or maybe a professor shaped your mental image of God. You sat in a class where some highly intelligent person with a string of degrees after his name insisted that God is a myth, and that shaped how you view God.

Or maybe your church formed your image of God. Whatever faith tradition you're from, this tradition painted a picture for you—sometimes good, sometimes not.

Or maybe your friends told you, by their actions or their words, *Hey, this is what God is like*, and that's influenced your thinking.

Or perhaps you have let your life experiences define God for you. Maybe in your mind God didn't come through for you, or He didn't hold up His side of a bargain you thought you'd made, or He disappointed you in some way—and that has shaped what you think of God.

I was reading recently about a pioneer in broadcast television who said he wanted nothing to do with God and considered himself an atheist because when he was younger and his father was dying, he prayed for his father's healing to no avail. If God was supposedly so good, then why didn't that good God save his dad? That one painful moment of confusion and disappointment shaped his view of God for the rest of his life.

The same can be said of us all. Something we learned, heard, or experienced has created an image in our minds of what we think God is like. While there are a multitude of views that people think about when they think about God, there are a few you run into more often than others.

A Motley Crew of Gods

Some people hold a mental image of God that looks something like an Old Man Upstairs—the **Grandpa God**. I'm not poking fun at anyone's concept of God. I'm just trying to be helpful by confronting what some of us think and taking the masks off some of our lesser gods. Grandpa God has been around forever, so it's no wonder he's moving a bit slower these days. He has a white flowing beard and a soothing Morgan Freeman–esque voice. He walks around heaven with a twinkle in his eye and a handful of candy. He's a little hard of hearing, so please speak up when you're trying to tell him something and, by all means, keep the racket down in the church.

Grandpa God is mostly out of touch with current culture and hasn't figured out how to text just yet. When he gets around to upgrading from a flip phone to a smartphone you can be sure he'll be using that super large font setting that the grandkids can read from across the room. He's gentle and kind, but he's certainly not going to be able to help you figure out the TV remote or the complex issues of today. He's a bit of a Santa, so be sure you leave some cookies out for him this year. Or maybe not.

Instead of a Grandpa God image, it could be that you see God as a rule-making, tally-keeping umpire in the sky.

Scorekeeper God is all about the dos and don'ts. If you go to church, you get one point. If you swear at the guy on the freeway who cuts you off, you lose two points. This god is always watching you, always evaluating, always judging, always working the numbers. He's constantly scribbling things about you in his ledger. Have a good thought? Noted. Have a bad attitude? Points come off the board. You've got to toe the line to stay in this god's good graces. You need to try hard if you want to stay on this god's team.

In the end, you stand outside the pearly gates, and this god hands you a computer-generated list of credits and debits. If you're lucky you have more credits than debits, and in you go. Hooray! With this god in mind, heaven is for folks who aren't in the red. You're only going to make it if you keep trying harder and you pile up enough good stuff to tip the scales in your favor.

Some see God as a nebulous force, some kind of positive energy or light. The **Cosmic Force God** is nameless and faceless, probably with no personhood or personality. This "force" is distant, abstract, and elusive. We might tap into it if all the variables are just so. It could be momentum. A feeling. A vibe. A harmonic convergence. When people have this image of God in mind, they often talk about spirituality yet they don't describe a god you can know personally. The emphasis with this god-concept is simply that there's something out there in the universe that's greater than we are, and for the most part it feels right and good. It's bright like light and quite mysterious and larger than us. But it's hard to be sure just what it is.

Your view of God may be a picture of a reckless brawler who's looking to pick a fight. **Angry God** loves to push people around, make them pay. Doling out punishment is his thing. Make no mistake, this god doesn't like you much. He can't wait to crush you with his thunderbolt of destruction. *Bammm!* Goodbye, you're toast.

If you're smart, you avoid Angry God, because, frankly, who wouldn't?! You went to this god's church once and noticed there weren't a lot of people there. Duh. This god isn't anybody you'd want to worship week after week. Why keep coming back for more of what he dishes out? He's just waiting for the perfect moment to smash you into smithereens.

For others, their god is akin to Alexa or Siri, those electronic helpers that computer gurus have cleverly invented. This god is a personal butler in the sky. **Concierge God** is at your beck and call twenty-four seven. Need directions? Just ask. Want to order some different weather? Done. Concierge God sends messages, checks your calendar, finds stuff, and gives you a funny answer to "What does the fox say?"

If you listen to the way some people talk about God, it's as if He exists only to work through their to-do list for them. You push a button and *poof,* he appears with a smile. But this god is never in your life for long. This god is highly convenient. You call on him only when help is needed. When you don't need him anymore, all you do is push a button again, and just like that, this god is gone.

The list goes on and on.

Stained Glass God is high browed and stoic. This god

uses complex theological words and prefers things buttoned up and proper. None of that "new" music in his church. This god might be handy if the occasion is a royal wedding. He prefers the super-uncomfortable, unpadded pews, and he's very concerned about the color of the carpet in the sanctuary. After all, it is *his* house. Some with this view think the church-house is where God *actually* lives.

Hipster God is super relevant—part barista, part Bible scholar.

Buddy God is on our level. We greet him with a casual "What's up, bro? High fives all around." He's chill and a good hang.

Crypto God is eager to drop a Bitcoin into your digital wallet.

The **Me God** is, well, *me*. Sure, we don't overtly say, *I'm God.* But we act like it. Or think like it. We call the shots. When this image of God is in our minds, everything is all about Me. Me. Me. I'm in charge. I make all the decisions. I'm in control. I'm self-made. The world revolves around me, and I steer my ship of destiny. Nobody tells me what to do, thank you very much.

Mash-Up God is a smorgasbord of all the above versions of God conveniently displayed so it's easy for you to pick and choose as you desire. This god is non-offensive, nonabrasive, and non-absolute. Nothing is ever considered right or wrong with this god. When this image of God is in your mind, you figure you can just walk up to the Great Salad Bar in the sky and pick and choose what to plunk on your plate. *I'll take a* *little bit of this and put it with a little bit of that.* This god might be everything, and this god might be nothing. You might be god, and I might be god, and all of us might be god, and nobody might be god.

Then, of course, there's the **No-God God**. It's actually hard to keep this image in mind because this image is actually a non-image. It's something you're trying to erase from your mind. You don't believe in God because you don't believe there's a God to believe in. I actually respect atheists quite a bit. I truly do. Every person on earth has to develop answers to the big questions of life—and then live by those answers. It takes real work and huge leaps of faith to answer those questions without God. But some try hard to do so and frame their existence based on a negative that cannot be proved, declaring, "There is no God."

Checking the Fingerprints of Creation

Granted, my descriptions of what people think God might be like are a little tongue in cheek. But it's likely you have a little bit of one of these views woven into your thinking. Or maybe your view of God is completely different. But whatever your answer is to the question, *What do you think about when you think about God?* the encouraging news is that God, the true God, is not sitting idly by in this conversation.

God wants you to know who He is. He's not hiding like a needle in a haystack, saying, "Good luck figuring out who I really am." He's not dropping you off in a spiritual corn maze, some kind of twisted game with eternal stakes. It's quite the opposite. God has surrounded you with His own fingerprints on His creation and overcome every possible hurdle to show you who He is and what He's like. More than you want to find God, God wants to be found by you.

He wants you to know Him and know how much He loves you.

That's why God is constantly in the process of revealing Himself. Through His Word, through creation, through the Holy Spirit at work in our lives, and yes, through the influence of godly people around us, God is constantly showing us who He is. God knows the stakes are high because if we don't know who He truly is, then we could spend our whole lives with the wrong idea of God, living out our days on earth trying to respond to a flawed image of God.

That can cause any number of problems. With a wrong view of God in mind, we can spend our lives running from the true God, or hiding from God, or angry at God, or disappointed with God, or feeling rejected by God, or ambivalent toward God, or worried we're on the wrong side of God's scorecard. That's not what the abundant life that Jesus offers to us looks like. And that's why we live in a universe that makes it impossible to miss Him.

When I was in college, my friend Johnny and I traveled across the United States camping in some of America's spectacular national parks. When we arrived at the Grand Canyon on a scorching July afternoon, we set our tent up in one of the campsites near the entrance to the national park. The view across the cavernous expanse was stunning, but what we really wanted to do was get to the bottom.

The problem was that reservations for the campsites down at the bottom of the canyon had to be booked months in advance. Sadly, we didn't have a reservation, so our options were limited. Hiking down and back up during the daytime was highly discouraged given the well above one-hundred-degree temperatures. The park ranger we'd asked for advice took a look at us and offered, "I don't think your odds are too good. You'll bake going down and wilt coming back up." But then she offered an intriguing possibility—we could hike down to the bottom during the night and then back out in the cooler morning hours.

"Sounds a little crazy," my buddy said, but after a few minutes he and I both arrived at the same conclusion and agreed we'd give it a shot.

Just after midnight, we started our descent of the Bright Angel Trail, slowly dropping into the canyon, led by the glow from our flashlights down the switchbacks that would take us far below the rim to the river's edge. Other than the few wild donkeys that startled us (I think they were more startled than we were) and what sounded like the rattle of a snake that definitely sped up our pace, things went according to plan, and we ended up on a little sandy beach by a bend in the Colorado River about four in the morning.

When we stretched out to catch a short nap before sunrise, I had no clue that my understanding of the majesty of God was about to change. As I looked up from the bottom of this mile-deep crevice in the earth (where there was no hint of man-made light), it was as if the stars were hanging so close you could pluck them out of the sky with your outstretched hand. They were like shimmering diamonds in the night sky, so brilliant against the black of space. I smiled.

And laughed. And actually reached for a few of them just to make sure I couldn't touch them. And I felt an overwhelming sense of awe and wonder that I had never known before. I believe that sense of mystery and greatness was the Creator blanketing the backdrop of the cosmos with the declaration, *I am here*. God certainly wasn't hiding that night. His glory was on display for all to see.

You may be thinking, *That sounds all well and good, Louie, but I have a friend who doesn't even believe in Jesus who would say something similar—that when she's out in nature that's when she communes with God and feels connected to the "divine universe." Yet her view of God doesn't sound a whole lot like yours!*

I get it. So how do we find an accurate view of God? How do we know which view is right and good? We begin by realizing God is constantly revealing Himself to us and that what we see of Him in the cosmos is just a starting place.

Coming into Focus

In Romans 1, God weighs in on Himself. He begins to define for us the image He wants to put in our minds. God wants to make sure we know who He is.

That which is known about God is evident within them; for God made it evident to them. For since the creation of the world His invisible attributes, that is, His eternal power and divine nature, have been clearly perceived, being understood by what has been made, so that they are without excuse. (vv. 19–20 NASB)

According to this passage, anybody, anywhere on planet Earth, can look up and look around and consider the universe—the mountains and waterfalls, the animals and sunsets, the stars and volcanoes, the marvelous flight-producing design of a feathered bird, the half a billion neurons in the motor cortex of your brain that are present just so you can talk—and conclude that there must be some divine force behind it all.

That's good news. Nature shows us that indeed there is a God, a creative, beautiful, intelligent God. And we can see evidence, like perfect fingerprints, of God all around us. For instance, not long ago, scientists used the Hubble Space Telescope to spot a galaxy they named GN-z11, the farthest galaxy we've ever seen. It's 13.4 billion light-years away from us,[7] and according to Romans 1, God's eternal power and divine nature can in fact be understood from what has been seen. Thanks to this galaxy far, far away—and many other evidences of God—people are "without excuse." When we consider that galaxy and the sheer craziness of how big the universe is, most people can't help but be drawn toward a divine being that is bigger than us all.

Besides leaving clues all over His creation, God gets even more specific in telling us what He's like. Hebrews 1:1–3 describes how the revelation process trickles down.

First, creation reveals God, as the Romans passage pointed out. Then the writer of Hebrews picks up the chain of events:

> In the past God spoke to our ancestors through the prophets at many times and in various ways, but in these last days he has spoken to us by his Son, whom he appointed heir of all things, and through whom also he made the universe. The Son is the radiance of God's glory and the exact representation of his being, sustaining all things by his powerful word.

The prophets of the Old Testament revealed God in a more specific way than even creation reveals Him. They pointed people to a coming Messiah, and that's where the funnel ends—with the coming of the Messiah, the person of Christ. Look at that phrase more closely—when Jesus, God's Son, stepped onto planet Earth, He was described as, "the radiance of God's glory and the *exact* representation of his being." In other words, Jesus showed us clearly who God is. God showed us who He is by sending Jesus, and Jesus was a walking, talking, living, breathing picture of God on earth.

Because God wanted you to have an unmistakably clear picture of what He is like, He sent Jesus into the pages of human history with this hope: "For God, who said, 'Let light shine out of darkness,' made his light shine in our hearts to give us the light of the knowledge of God's glory displayed in the face of Christ" (2 Corinthians 4:6).

Don't miss these two powerful truths:

God has given us the light of the knowledge of His glory.

This knowledge of God's glory is found in the face of Christ.

That's what we're going to camp on a lot in this book, because we want to consider how amazing this is. Jesus' life is recorded in the pages of Scripture, partially so we can know what He did and stood for and came to offer the world, and partially so we can know what a glorious God looks like. Jesus sketched on the canvas a picture of who God is for all of us to see and understand so we can respond to God in the right way.

Now, when Scripture says in Hebrews that Jesus is the "exact representation" of God's being, that doesn't mean that God is a smiling five-foot-eight, dark-haired, bearded Jewish man with a lamb in His arms. It means that if we look at the heart of Christ, the mind of Christ, the attitude of Christ, the way Christ treated people, the things He said, the way He lived, the way He valued the world and all things in it, we'll see in Jesus a picture of what God is like.

This is so key for us to grasp. In Jesus, God most clearly says, "Here I am. Here's the most accurate picture I can give you of what I'm like." The Tozer quote I mentioned earlier, which I first heard from Dan DeHaan, has been driving my life in my relationship with God for a long time, and I realized long ago that if I want to answer Dan's question with any kind of accuracy, then I need to look at Jesus. The life and death of this peasant from Nazareth teaches us so much about God— that God is powerful, holy, omnipotent, ruler of all things, greater than all things, loving, saving, good, generous, compassionate, and much more.

Yet there is something even more amazing that Jesus teaches us about God, and it's a revolutionary truth that sets us free to become everything God created us to be. The number one image of God that Jesus paints for us again and again is that God is a *Father*. He is our perfect Abba Father.

Did you catch that? Of all the things that Jesus teaches us about God, the big idea He's seeking to get across to us is that God is a *Father*. God wants you to know Him, and He invites you to call Him Father. He wants you to know you can live as a loved son, a loved daughter.

Can I say that again? God wants you to know that you can live as a dearly loved son, a dearly loved daughter.

And He wants you to live under the waterfall of His blessing. Jesus shows us this both in His teaching and in His relationship with His Father. Let's follow this road map to develop a right-side-up view of God. After all, who better to give us that right view of God than His own Son?

Chapter 3

A God to Call Father

A few years ago I was flying home to Atlanta after speaking at an event in Texas. I boarded the plane and settled into my seat in 2C. This particular plane was a smaller regional jet with two seats on each side of the aisle, front to back. I was in the aisle seat on row two on the right side of the plane facing the cockpit. I always aim to be the last person to board, so once I made it to my seat, it was odd to see the flight crew standing idle as our departure time came and went. Pretty soon I figured out (from bits of the conversation I overheard) that we were waiting for another passenger.

I noticed seat 1B was empty and my mind began to race with the possibilities. What important VIP were we waiting on? Maybe it was an entertainer, a well-known politician, an actor, or a famous athlete.

We waited, and I watched the front of the plane. Most people sitting around me were oblivious to what was happening, clueless to the fact that an online tabloid moment was about to happen. The lady across the aisle was captivated by her Sudoku puzzle, and the guy next to me was already sound asleep. But my eyes stayed glued.

Finally, I heard commotion in the jetway and then he appeared!

Hmmm. That's the guy we've been waiting for? I thought. I didn't recognize him. A guy in his late twenties rounded the corner and plopped his messenger bag down in the seat. He wore medical scrubs. *Who is this guy? Why have we waited for him?*

Then I saw he had a small Styrofoam container under his left arm, about the size of an old-school toaster. I was thinking, *Who brings a Styrofoam chest through security and onto a plane?* That's when I noticed the decals on each side of the container: *Human Eyes.*

I'm sure my eyes opened wide as he casually opened the overhead bin, slid a lady's sweater to the side, shoved the container in, along with his messenger bag, and slammed the compartment shut. He slumped into his seat, fastened his seat belt, and promptly dozed off.

Everything about this unnerved me. I was arrested by the fact that someone had lost their life. I didn't know any details, their age, or the circumstances of their death. But I knew that the person had been an organ donor, and their eyes were now in that container. I also knew that my seatmate's role on the transplant team was to rush those eyes to an operating room where a hopeful patient was waiting. I didn't know anything about the patient either, except that they needed sight. But mostly my eyes were riveted on the overhead bin. What if the bin somehow popped open during a patch of turbulence?

As far as I could tell I was the only person paying enough attention to know there were human eyes in the storage compartment above row one! I felt totally responsible for the safe passage of this precious cargo, but soon after takeoff it was business as usual inside the cabin.

"Would you like something to drink? Some pretzels or peanuts?" the flight attendant offered.

"No," I blurted, diverting my eyes from the bin for only a fraction of a second. How could I have a snack when there were human eyes in that overhead bin?!

I stayed transfixed. Once we landed and pulled up to our gate, the man popped opened the bin. Thankfully, the container with the eyes was still there. He grabbed up his gear and was the first one off the plane. But I was pretty close behind. Not within stalking distance, but close enough.

When we reached the midpoint of the concourse, I knew my car, my arriving baggage, and my house were toward the right, but I went left, following the eyes down the escalator and onto the train. I didn't get in the same train car, but I could see my man through the glass window at the end of my car. I was still in contact with the eyes.

The guy and the eyes were headed to Knoxville. I knew this because that's what it said at gate C-22 where he was waiting for his connecting flight. I sat across the wide walkway in an adjoining gate, praying for the family of the person from which the eyes had come and praying for the surgical procedure that would bring so much joy to the person and family receiving this precious gift.

Once the flight boarded I walked to the wall of windows nearby. They pulled the jetway back from the plane, and the door was closed. The Knoxville flight backed away from the gate, and a sense of relief flooded over me. The eyes were safely on their way to Tennessee.

Maybe my actions seem silly, but I really did feel an attachment to the mission of getting those eyes to their intended destination. I headed to baggage claim and gathered my suitcase from the luggage carousel and headed home, all the while thinking in amazement: *Someone in Knoxville, Tennessee, is going to see today!* Because of the death of one person, sight was coming to another. The corneal transplant that was about to take place in Knoxville was going to bring clarity of vision to a person who hadn't been able to see for a season, or maybe for their entire life.

Someone in Knoxville was going to see! What a miraculous day this was going to be!

In the same way, I'm writing this today in hopes of another miracle of sight—that moment when the Spirit of God opens someone's eyes to see what Jesus was showcasing through His teachings and His relationship with His Father. To see that God wants us to know Him.

This is how the apostle Paul described it as he was praying for some of the first believers in Jesus: "I keep asking that the God of our Lord Jesus Christ, the glorious Father, may give you the Spirit of wisdom and revelation, so that you may know him better. I pray that the eyes of your heart may be enlightened" (Ephesians 1:17–18).

That's my prayer for you and me as we are talking about the possibility of seeing God as a perfect Father. I'm praying that God will give us a spirit of revelation by opening the eyes of our hearts so we can know Him more.

We've already talked about some faulty views of God, but even when leafing through the pages of Scripture, it's possible to end up missing the point and *not see* the main image of who He is. If we hold too narrow of an image, even though it's found in Scripture, it can still skew how we think of God and how we respond to Him. Our image needs to be biblical, and our image needs to be balanced according to how Scripture weighs the various images and words used to describe God.

I've already given you a sneak peek at the primary mental image of God that Scripture shows us, the image that Jesus points to again and again. Keep in mind, this is not the *only* image of God presented in Scripture. It's the *main* image of God. The chief image. The principal image. The key image. This is the image we need to direct our primary response mechanism toward.

Watch closely, because what follows is going to sound suspect if you gloss over this concept too quickly or don't follow it through to the end. The number one image of God that Jesus draws for us again and again is something *different* from all the things in the following list.

It's not that God is King.
It's not that He's the Ruler of the universe.
It's not that He's the God of justice.

It's not that He's the Alpha and Omega, the beginning
and the end.

It's not that He's the Rock, the God of faithfulness and
steadfastness.

It's not that He's the hope of eternal life.

It's not that He's immortal, invisible, the only wise God.

It's not that He's the Creator of the heavens and the earth.

It's not that He's a merciful God.

It's not that He's the Logos, the Word that became flesh
and dwelt among us.

It's not that He's the great I AM.

It's not that He's the Lord, the God of Israel.

It's not that He's the Lord of Hosts.

It's not that He's our redeemer.

It's not that He's a mighty warrior.

It's not that He's the owner of the cattle on a
thousand hills.

It's not that He's light.

It's not that He's the wonderful Counselor, mighty God,
Prince of Peace.

It's not that He's the one who is high and lifted up, who
inhabits eternity, whose name is Holy.

It's not even that He's love.

God is not primarily any *one* of these things alone. And
this gets straight to the heart of what I want to focus on. To
be clear, *God is all of those images and realities in the above list.*
All of those images and realities come straight from Scripture,

and all are true about God. Yet none of those are emphasized by Jesus as often as something else. Jesus repeated it over and over and drove this characteristic of God into our souls. The number one image of God that Jesus drew for us again and again is this:

God is a Father.

The Father Is Near

Both through His relationship with His Father and His teaching, Jesus wants us to see God in a new way. Jesus is saying God is powerful and majestic and glorious and full of wisdom and grace and truth—and yes, He's all these things—but there's more. Get this: all of God's characteristics are wrapped in the person of a Father. It helps us so much to see God this way, because so many of God's attributes are difficult for us to grasp. For example, the essence of justice. Justice is merely a concept, and it's hard to put our arms around a concept. But we can embrace a just Father. Further, it can be hard for us to embrace grace and truth. These are wonderful concepts, but only concepts. Yet we can embrace a Father who is full of grace and truth.

God is relatable. He's knowable. Because the fatherhood of God is the main characteristic that holds all His other attributes together.

Don't take my word for it. Listen to the words of Jesus. Time after time, in some of the most well-known parts of

His teaching, Jesus draws our attention to God in a very specific way.

Once Jesus chose His inner circle of disciples, He quickly showed them how to pray. Surprisingly, He opened His model prayer with some words that must have sounded unbelievable to the disciples' ears. Jesus didn't begin His prayer with "Dear sir," or "Your Majesty," or even "Most Holy Lord." No. Jesus said in Matthew 6 that when you talk to God, you start by saying,

"Our Father . . ."

Jesus immediately affirmed for them that God is not just any old kind of father when He continued:

". . . in heaven, hallowed be your name."

Yet He reframed the God of the Old Testament faith, a God no one could approach, as Father.

Later, in that same message, Jesus talked about how to best live. He said faith in action is like a light that you set on a hill, so you can give glory to who? Your spiritual boss? No. To the "man upstairs"? No. Jesus said, "Let your light shine before others, that they may see your good deeds and glorify your Father in heaven" (Matthew 5:16). In other words, we're invited to live in such a way that the world doesn't merely see that we do good things but that we do good things because we're in a relationship with a perfect Father.

In John 14:6, Jesus provided one of the clearest explanations of what it means to live in relationship with the Father. Jesus said, "I am the way and the truth and the life. No one comes to the *Father* except through me" (emphasis added).

And in John 14:9, Jesus said these ultra-clear words: "Don't you know . . . Anyone who has seen me has seen the *Father*" (emphasis added).

We find this type of clarifying-father-understanding again and again in the teachings of Jesus. In fact, 189 times in the four Gospels alone, Jesus referred to God as a Father, far more than any other term, distinction, or characteristic Jesus used to describe Him. Even when Jesus was dying on the cross, with His last breath He said, "*Father*, into your hands I commit my spirit" (Luke 23:46, emphasis added).

This is how we come to know and embrace and relate to the almighty One. We come to see God as a heavenly Father.

We see this not only in the way Jesus relates with His Father, but also in the newsworthy declaration of the Father about His Son. One of the first places in Scripture that the Fatherhood of God was displayed was in Matthew 3 when Jesus came to John the Baptist to be baptized. There was John, ribcage-deep in the Jordan River, his camelhair clothes sopping wet.

He was baptizing people right and left as he preached and prepared the way for the Lord. Suddenly, up walked Jesus, saying, "Hey, baptize Me." And John was like, "Wah-what? You got that backward, Jesus. You need to baptize me!" So they talked back and forth, but finally John relented and plunged Jesus into the Jordan River and brought Him up again. Jesus was baptized to identify with sinners in their redemption, new and clean. Scripture says that when Jesus came up out of the water, the heavens opened, the Holy Spirit descended like a dove and alighted on Jesus, and a voice from heaven gave a startling and altogether wonderful announcement. Do you know what it was?

The announcement was big news to all those gathered by the Jordan that day. Many of the folks who were gathered around John the Baptist must have already known this thirty-year-old man, Jesus of Nazareth. He was Joseph's kid, the carpenter's son. Jesus had grown up in a little village not far away. They must have remembered Him playing as a boy, running down the side streets. They'd seen Him in the synagogue and marketplace, fully grown. And now, after Jesus was baptized by John, God the Father went on record, speaking in an audible voice at the baptism service.

And what exactly did God say?

"Hey everyone, sorry I'm late but I was at the AARP Convention. Did the kid do okay?"

Or, "Hey boy, You better get in that river and get dunked like I told You to."

Or, "Can't you just feel a sense of peace and tranquility in the universe today?"

Nope.

The Father calls out: "THIS IS MY SON, WHOM I LOVE! WITH HIM I AM WELL PLEASED!"

It's like He was saying, "I'm God, and that's My kid! I love Him a lot. With Him I am well pleased." How crazy is that? If God's going to call down from heaven, surely He's going to give a full sermon. Surely He'll dazzle us with His theological omniscience.

Nope.

Just simple fatherly delight.

We need to soak in that concept. We need to stay there, to bask in it, to enjoy it. See, by the Jordan River that day, God the Father showed that His relationship with Jesus wasn't a contract. It wasn't the signing of a theological treatise. It wasn't a list of principles to agree with or a bunch of rules to follow. It was a connection. A family connection. A real, heart-to-heart life connection where the Creator of the universe acknowledged His Son. Yes, God is all knowing and all powerful and all wise, and He's holy and just and perfect, and there is a just wrath awaiting those who reject His truth and grace. But here's what Jesus reveals most about Him—God is a loving Father. We see it clearly as God the Father pulled back the curtain and showed us this amazing relationship with the Son whom He dearly loves. And God extends a similar kind of relationship to us. A relationship where He is our Father and we are His sons and daughters. God loves us, and God is even proud to call us His own. Let that fact sink in a bit.

Huge, Enormous, Jolting Image

That's the big hope of this book—that when I say God, you will think *Father*. That's the image that will come to mind. Yes, I want you to think holy. And mighty. And glorious. But all in the context of Father.

Our identity as sons and daughters of God unlocks prison doors, heals wounds, and

propels us into greater purpose in our lives.

I know this *father* concept can send us spinning in any number of ways. For some it's an immediate hurdle, a barrier one hundred feet high. When you hear that God is a father you may instantly think, *No thank you. I don't want any of that. If God is like my father, then I'm out.*

Wait. I plead with you to stay with me as we slowly take a look at this idea and spend some time gently peeling back the layers of our hearts in several of the next chapters. We all have earthly fathers, and some of those fathers were good, and some of them were not so good. Our mental image of what a father is like is mostly influenced by our earthly fathers. I know this, and I get this, and I want to be sensitive to you and what you've been through and are going through with your dad. I don't want to minimize in any way what's happening right now when I say "father."

Please know if that word pushes on a nerve or exposes a hurt, I'm not doing that without a lot of grace and care. I want to give you room to cry, to be mad, to set the book down and think for a while—to wonder and ponder and journal and take your time processing what God is saying to you. Yet I also want to resolutely and lovingly and biblically point you to this amazing truth: that the knowledge of our identity as sons and daughters of God unlocks prison doors, heals wounds, and propels us into greater purpose in our lives.

When we know that God is our perfect Father, and we live out of the revolutionizing identity this new awareness gives us, we can come alive in this truth. Old things pass away— disappointments, guilt, sorrows, and struggles. Habits change for the better. Our relationship with God is transformed. Our worship is revived. We see changes in the things we long for and hope for, and how we see other people is affected.

Broken Relationships

I know that it might be a stretch for you right now to think of God as your Father or to envision that He loves you and is delighted to call you His son or daughter.

Right now, I'm thinking about a friend whose dad left for another life with another woman when she was young. Her father said it was about "finding himself" and that he and her mom were moving in different directions. Her dad ended up in a new city, with a new job, and ultimately with a new family. First it was a new girlfriend, but eventually he found another woman who became his new wife. Everything was beginning again for him while his daughter was left behind to figure out what happened and to pick up the pieces of her heart.

Her dad had sat her down when he broke the news that he was moving out. *Moving on.* And then he emphasized, "It's not about you, it's about me. You must realize this is not about you, sweetheart, this is about Dad!"

Yet, as he spoke, her mind inverted his words from *this is not about you,* to *this is all about me.*

She told me that at first the lines of communication between them were steady, but in time the calls got less and less frequent and then became mostly texts. Eventually, there was mostly silence. Not malicious silence. Just the deafening quiet that underscored the emerging reality that she wasn't that important to her dad after all. For her dad the silence was always explained as *being busy*. But to her the silence was translated *unseen, unwanted—that she wasn't a priority any-more*. It made her wonder if he ever did love her—if she ever had a place in his heart.

In time, she built up walls to hide the pain and protect her heart. She tried to stuff the anger and ended up trusting no one. She became lost in so many protective emotional lay-ers she didn't even know who she was. At the time she was telling me all this she was confiding to our team that she was struggling with an eating disorder and was in and out of unhealthy relationships with guys. She was dying on the inside.

For her, the instinctive desire for a father's love and approval had crashed and burned. She had the kind of dad who didn't see her and appreciate her and want her. Her primal need for her dad's arms to be strong and his heart to be good was left unfilled, and her heart was withering away in the face of his failure. As time went on she wasn't sure if her dad's arms were strong or not, but more and more it didn't seem like his heart was good. Either he was defective or she was. Or both.

I'm also thinking about a high-achieving leader who came to me for advice recently. He was thinking he'd stuffed the long-standing resentment he held toward his father for the way he was treated all his life far away in the Never Never Land of forgetfulness. Yet now he was confiding in me as a successful businessman leading a great family and living miles away from his dad—both emotionally and geographically—that the fire of bitterness was consuming his thoughts and polluting his relationships. Though he'd tried his best to erase the past and walk away, he couldn't break free from the way his dad had made him feel about himself.

Still another friend was robbed of his dad by death at an early age. As we were talking about a father's approval, he just stared into space with no real concept of what we were discussing. When we talked about living with a father's blessing over our lives, this friend just continued to stare into the distance. He can only wonder what it must be like to grow up under the shadow of that kind of love and approval from a father that is his own flesh and blood.

As I write, I am thinking about you and of the father relationships that could have been better, or even existent, in your life. I can understand if the feelings running through your heart right now as we talk about God being a father are not positive but painful. Not hopeful but hurtful. Not redemptive but more like a wrecking ball crashing into things you just might prefer to leave walled up in the past. If that's you, I believe God may have placed this book in your hands to reverse the curse of "what has been" and transform everything about you.

Tribute to an Imperfect Dad

Not all the thoughts that are rushing through people's minds as we say the word *father* are painful.

For example, my wife, Shelley, had an amazing dad. He was a strong, loving, supportive dad who championed her, prayed for her, and modeled strength, integrity, and consistency for her until his recent death. And it's not just Shelley who has received the benefit of his goodness. Her dad was a great father to me as well.

Yet the more stories I hear, the more I realize fathers like this are less and less common in today's generation.

I was blessed to have an amazing earthly father who I can be proud of. You met him in the story I told earlier about our conversation by the kitchen stove. Like all dads, he wasn't perfect, but he tried to be the best dad he could be.

He died a while back. His name was also Louie Giglio. (Actually, my grandfather had the same name, too, so I'm Louie Giglio III.) My dad was a graphic designer, and he had a brilliant mind.

Back in 1964 my dad designed the Chick-fil-A logo, and it's been printed on every one of their cups, wrappers, napkins, and signs since then. My sister (who was his favorite between the two of us) saw an early draft while sitting on the sofa in our den. At the time, he was working freelance for a man who ran an advertising firm in Atlanta, and Chick-fil-A was one of his clients. That particular night Dad was tweaking their "Chicken C." Gina, seven years old at the time, told my dad she thought it was "so cute."

How cool is that?!

A few years ago the CEO of Chick-fil-A told me that they'd hired multiple ad agencies since then, most all of which wanted to update the Chick-fil-A image. But that one little logo has endured through the decades with only slight modifications. My dad's little $75 creation has stood the test of time. When I look at that logo, I think: *Yep, my dad did that!*

But I'm not surprised. My dad was a genius.

He was an original.

He was a true artist.

He was a lover of music and could build a killer stereo system from scratch.

He was a captivating storyteller.

He was a golf fanatic. He loved the legends like Ben Hogan, Arnold Palmer, and Jack Nicklaus, but he was an enormous fan of the South African, Gary Player. Many afternoons as I was growing up, we would head to a nearby putting green or driving range to hit some golf balls after he got off work. When going to a real putting green wasn't an option, we would hold fierce putting competitions on the carpeted floors of our apartment, using furniture legs or glasses from the kitchen for the holes.

Dad was an Auburn grad, earning his art degree in the football national championship year, 1957. He taught me how to root for the Tigers and say "War Eagle." And in the old days when games were mostly on the radio, we'd sit together with my sister, and when Auburn would score to win the game we'd run *on the furniture*, from chair to sofa to coffee table, and yell as loud as we could!

He worked hard to provide for us.

Dad drank a little and sometimes a lot.

He definitely was not a planner.

He was a nonconformist.

He had the most expansive vocabulary. He could turn a phrase in a clever way. For example, he would tell us before we went to sleep, "Don't bite the bed bugs" instead of "Don't let the bed bugs bite."

He'd give you the shirt off his back if you needed it.

He treated everyone the same, no matter who they were or where they were from.

Dad served in the Korean War as a mapmaker.

His first real job out of Auburn was in Atlanta (that's where I came along), and that's where he's buried.

And what about my dad's dad—Louie Giglio I? I don't have a clue what he was like. My granddad died suddenly before my dad was thirty, and though I'm a namesake of my grandfather, I have no memory of him. Dad rarely mentioned him, if at all.

My dad was an only child, and due to the instability between his mom and dad, and most likely the lifestyle that caused my grandfather Louie to die young, my dad was shuffled between family members when he was little. He learned quickly how to fend for himself and build up walls. He attended all three high schools in his town in a four-year stretch.

In the last chapter of his life, after being ravaged by a rare viral infection in his brain resulting in him being disabled mentally and physically, Dad confided in me words that echo in my mind to this day:

"No one ever loved me."

"No one wanted me."

"And I know God doesn't love me either."

That's where we were toward the end of his life. This brilliant man, and good father, telling me that he believed no one ever wanted him.

I was stunned, tears welling up in my eyes. Slowly, it began dawning on me that my dad was a person too.

I wanted to blurt out, "You are loved, you are wanted by me, Dad. By me! By us!"

But the pain was deep. And the wound had been lingering for decades. For the first time I began to realize my father wasn't only a dad, he was also a son—a broken son. Here we sat all these years later and whatever it was that went down between my father and his father sixty years before was still the dominant story in the room.

I wondered if my dad hadn't become disabled and experienced such traumatic changes in his brain if I would ever have known the pain he'd been carrying all those years. Would I have ever understood how the lack of a father's blessing had crashed into his life and, in turn, into mine?

Given all that, it's incredible the way he loved and cared for my sister and me. In spite of his shattered sense of self, he was a pretty darn good dad. And I miss him.

But my "father story" doesn't end with "Big Lou." I also have a heavenly Father in my life.

The Only Perfect Father

As proud as I am of my earthly dad, I'm infinitely more amazed by my heavenly Father. I can hardly conceive of the reality that, through Christ, I've been graced to become a son of the heavenly Father. I am a child of almighty God. When I see a sunrise, or the Alps, or images of a galaxy that's 13.4 billion light-years away, I think: *Wow, my heavenly Father did that. And He knows my name. I belong to Him. He might not have designed the "chicken-headed" Chick-fil-A logo, but my heavenly Father actually created the chicken and everything else in creation!*

The same can be true of you. This relationship becomes yours when you trust in God through Jesus Christ. God brings your heart to life, and you are born anew as a son or daughter of a perfect heavenly Father. This spiritual birth not only brings us to life on the inside, it places us in a new family with a new Father. When Jesus was on the cross, He used a specific word that I hope sticks in our souls. When crying out to God, Jesus called Him *Abba.*

Abba is Aramaic, the common language of Jesus' day. It was the word little kids used when addressing their earthly dads. Abba isn't perfectly translated into English as *Daddy* or *Papa,* but it's close to that: a word that's tender, affectionate, easy for a child to say. The word connotes confidence in a father. It's not a formal title. It's a familiar title. It's what a child says when he knows he's close to his father and that his father is close to him.

In Romans 8:15, the Bible says we, as believers, can use

this same title when addressing God: *Abba*. That means God isn't some kind of nebulous force impossible to know or understand. He's not your great cosmic butler in the sky. He doesn't live in a stained glass cathedral; He isn't keeping score on you, and He's not merely your buddy. God is not a bully or a grandpa or the face you look at in the mirror.

God is a Father. And through Christ, God can be your *Abba*, Father.

This is the God Jesus taught us about and the image I'm inviting you to see and know deep within your soul and keep there for always. It's an image that's truth, and it's an image that shapes everything. This is what I hope becomes the most important thing about you—that you would know without a doubt that God is your Father and that you are a beloved child of God.

If that image is hard or painful for you, or maybe if you're simply wondering what this God-as-a-Father business is all about, you'll soon see that you've been given a surprise gift.

But it's nothing like you ever expected.

Chapter 4

Reflection Versus Perfection

One of the things Shelley and I were looking forward to most when moving from the suburbs to the city was the panoramic view of the downtown skyline we would enjoy from the rooftop of our new townhouse. Granted, you had to take the utility stairs and be a bit of a risk-taker to get to the roof of our building, but that didn't dampen my enthusiasm in the slightest. We had a stunning city view! That is, until the vacant lot next door became home to a condo building that ended up being eleven feet taller than our rooftop. Just tall enough to completely obstruct our skyline view.

In the same way, your earthly dad may be responsible for erecting an image of Father that is impeding your view of a loving heavenly Father.

Discovering that God wants to be known as a perfect Father is only half of the journey. Each of us has a picture of what a father is like that's primarily based on our relationship with our earthly dads. Although God is loving and inviting and trustworthy and dependable, it's as if something—or someone—constructed a barrier that makes it difficult to take in this amazing aspect of God's character. Our view is being blocked by a flawed understanding of what a father is.

That's the challenge inherent in declaring that *God is a Father.* All of our earthly fathers have fallen short, some more than others. Some fathers proved themselves true—time and time again. But others proved false—and this also happened time and time again. Let's face it. There's a fatherhood crisis in our world. According to the National Fatherhood Initiative, one in four kids lives in a home without a dad.[8] That's a quarter of the children in the US waking up each day without any type of father present in their lives. Yet such a staggering realization shouldn't come as a surprise.

The Enemy seeks to destroy fatherhood. He wants to break apart our image of what a good father is. He wants to destroy families and wreck the relationships between fathers and their kids. If he can shatter our picture of good earthly fathers, then he might in turn blast our image of our perfect heavenly Father. And if the Enemy can't completely shatter our image of God, maybe he can mess with it just enough to keep us from living fully free.

Six Fathers

I don't pretend to know or fully understand what your dad was/is like. But there are six father figures that tend to dominate our stories. Maybe your dad is like one of these or has characteristics of a couple of them.

The Absent Father

This father could be absent due to death, divorce, distance, or disinterest. He may have been gone before you even took your first breath. Or maybe you knew him, but some disease, or accident, or violence took him from you. If he is around today, maybe he's too busy or he's moved on to another life, another family, another city.

The bottom line: he's not present in your life.

When Dad is gone there's a void, a hole. Whether we admit it or not, we're left to compensate for the absence of everything that's good about having a dad. The blessing. The physical hug. The support. The words *I love you, and you are mine.*

Without a dad who is present in our world, the sense of security we need isn't there. The protection every son and daughter longs for is missing. All you're left with are questions: *Why did my dad have to die? God, why did You do this to me?*

If he's still alive but vacant from our stories, we ask: *Why did he disappear on me? Am I just not that important to him? Does he even know I exist? Is he ashamed of me? What did I do wrong?*

So, when you hear "God wants you to know Him as your father," you think, *Hoo boy, that must mean He's not interested in me at all. How can I know He's gonna stay? For all I know He'll just walk away.*

Often, the void left by an absent father causes us to build a shell around our hearts, seemingly impenetrable armor that protects us from ever feeling that sense of loss and pain and betrayal again.

But it's hard to shake the "abandoned" or "orphaned" tag, and it's a massive challenge for any of us who've been left behind not to overcompensate for the loss of a father's blessing by claiming our worth from a thousand lesser things. It's hard to walk free from the absence of one of the things we needed most.

The Abusive Father

If this was your father, then you have known a barrage of killing words, cutting words, defaming words, debilitating words.

Maybe you felt the brunt of emotional abuse. You were condemned, humiliated, intimidated, manipulated, always kept off-kilter. The actions of your father chipped away at your dignity and destroyed your self-worth. For some it was verbal abuse. You were constantly yelled at, threatened, cursed. Or maybe you were physically abused. You were punched, kicked, shoved, thrown around, or your family members were physically hurt in front of you. Abuse may have been sexual. Maybe your dad did or said horrible things to you that undermined your sense of privacy and dignity and made you feel disgusting inside. Maybe the abuse was spiritual. Your dad led you in harmful spiritual directions.

Or he coerced or condemned or conned you with his spirituality.

Whatever form the abuse took, you were always wondering

where you stood, and maybe you grew up depressed, anxious, defensive, angry, maybe even suicidal.

If a father's abuse is in your story, it's possible your trust level is low, especially toward men or anyone in a position of authority. You've been cheated of innocence and robbed of self-worth. Life was a daily game of survival and you learned how to survive with the best of them.

For some people, survival happens by creating an alter ego, delegating the abuse to another version of themselves. Some harbor a raging fire of anger that consumes them from the inside out—bitterness toward the abuser and intense frustration toward themselves for letting it happen.

Emotions are not easily accessed or shared with others. Isolation becomes the norm. Close relationships tend to burn out because intimacy and vulnerability are always just out of reach.

I've talked with people who were abused by their fathers, and strangely enough, some say that at the time of the abuse they didn't put all the blame on their dad. They actually thought something about them was the problem. Surely, they must have done something wrong or been defective in some way to receive that kind of treatment. (Answer: no!) Abuse can be weakening and crippling, and it can drive a serious blow to a person's sense of identity, confidence, and worth. If God is like this, why would anyone want to be near Him?

The Passive Father

This dad might be a nice guy, but he's weak and mostly silent. He refused to take up the mantle of leadership in your family. Mom ran the show while Dad sat quietly by. With this dad there's no initiative, no responsibility, no guidance, no action. Dad is paralyzed. Perhaps he's on the couch with the remote in his hand, or perhaps he's frozen by some trauma in his past that's undisclosed. He's not abusive, and he's always there, but he's a nonfactor in the day-to-day decisions and struggles of your life.

He's defeated, perhaps steamrolled into submission by some events in his life. Ultimately, he can't be the father you so desperately want him to be. And he has never shown you how to live—how to face an uncertain world with confidence and courage. He's never shown you as a son how to be a man. He's never modeled for you as a daughter what it looks like to be loved and treasured by a man who honors and serves you and will fight for you.

This father never set any real ground rules. Never showed you tough love. You always did whatever you wanted as far as Dad was concerned. And, while you told your friends you loved the freedom his disinterest afforded you, you really wanted your dad to care enough to say, *Enough, stop.*

If God is like this dad, then perhaps He, too, is a nonfactor in your life. Honestly, you don't need Him.

The Performance-Based Father

Life with this dad is a grind. He's fine with handing out the blessing—the love, the approval, the encouragement—but it all comes with conditions. With this dad you have to earn his love. Only if you run faster than the other kids, you might get a high five at the end of the race. Only if you get straight As, you might hear "job well done." Only if you act a certain way, or achieve a certain position, or measure up to a certain standard, you might receive this dad's approval. Jump through the preset hoops, you get the hug. Ring the bell, you get the love. But if you stumble or fall, if you make a misstep along the way, you'll hear about it. And you'll pay the price.

Withheld love is used as a motivator. And for some that works to a degree. They jump higher. Achieve more. Try harder. Always doing whatever it takes to make Dad happy. They may resent Dad's ways, but some end up spending their entire life proving to him that they were good enough all along.

For others, living with this father leaves them feeling crippled, beaten down. Eventually, afraid to fail and sure they will never get it right, they just cave in and give up. *I'll never be good enough for him,* they think. *What's the point in trying anymore?*

This dad is always watching you, always evaluating, often condemning, often judging. This father helps you only when you help yourself. And if God the Father is like this earthly dad, then you always feel like you have to do more. You have to earn your way into God's approval. If you ever mess up, you're finished. No thanks.

The Antagonistic Father

Instead of giving you the blessing, this dad is always giving you a run for your money. He first reminds you that you're not all that great, and then he sets out to prove why he's better than you. This father always puts you on the defensive. He's your sparring partner, but it goes way beyond fun and games. He's your adversary, your nemesis, a hostile presence. Then he sets himself up to compete for all the attention. He soaks up all the oxygen in the room.

He points out all your flaws to others and plants failure in your mind every time you try something new. He's not for you. He's against you. And before you can ever have the chance of succeeding out in the world, you have to fight your way out of your own home.

Surely God who sent His Son into the world is not a Father like this.

The Empowering Father

Some of you know that although your dad's not perfect, he's doing his best. Your dad is or was a really good father, and whether he's still present in your life, or death has taken him from you, his blessing is a big part of who you're becoming. There are more than a few dads like this in the world.

This father is a kind, strong, encouraging dad. When it comes to loving his family, this father is the one who constantly does his best. He might still wear Bermuda shorts with dark socks and dress shoes when he goes to the mall, but he's always telling his kids he loves them. He's the guy who makes every attempt to be there for his children.

Are you fortunate enough to know a good father? This dad, when you were little, stuck his head inside your bedroom door at night and said, "Hey, I just want you to know I love you. You're my favorite son!" You smiled as you heard him say those same words to your brother down the hall.

As you grew older, he provided a safety net that allowed you the security to reach for things you never dreamed you could reach for. He's the dad who, if you messed up or failed, you could still call. In fact, he's the first person you called.

His love wasn't without correction when you needed it. But you always knew it really did hurt him more than it hurt you when he needed to discipline you.

He is your hero, your role model. And he has shown you how good it is to know that God is a Father too. Someone you can trust, depend on, and imitate.

Not long ago I was officiating the wedding of a twenty-something couple in our church. Just as the ceremony was about to begin, I witnessed something special.

While I didn't know the parents of the bride and groom all that well, I did know they both came from strong, loving families. I'd heard that the groom's dad was outspoken about his love for Jesus, and that he would openly and enthusiastically tell every restaurant server, rideshare driver, bystander, or neighbor about the great love of God. So what happened next as the groom and I were about to walk down the aisle was no surprise. Yet it was incredibly powerful.

Standing on the porch of a beautiful estate home, Josh and I were just a few minutes away from taking our place under the massive pecan tree at the end of the path between the guests. Josh's brothers and his dad were behind us when his father raised his voice in our direction.

"I love you, son!" he shouted out.

"God bless Josh! God bless Louie! Glory to God. All praise to Jesus. Oh, praise you Jesus. Glory to God."

"God bless Josh," he continued. "God bless Louie."

As we started moving toward the altar, I could hear Josh's dad in the distance saying, "Glory to God! God bless Josh!"

What a powerful picture of an empowering father.

Josh literally was under the waterfall of his father's blessing every step of the way toward one of the biggest moments of his life.

If you've had a father like that, you most likely have a head start toward seeing God as Father. But if you've lived with one of these other types of dads, or some hybrid of a few of them, you may feel like you're still stuck. Stuck with a twisted view of *father* that's making it difficult for you to embrace this idea that God wants you to know Him as Abba Father.

Everything You've Ever Dreamed

So, where do you go from here if your view of *father* has been shattered? How do you move forward if your trust in the one who should have been the most trustworthy person in your life (your earthly dad) has been damaged or corrupted or blurred? How can you celebrate the fact that there is a great God in heaven who wants you to know Him as Abba? If God is a father like yours, why would you want anything to do with Him?

Well, here's the good news—the life-altering news I've been waiting to share since we started this book:

God is not the *reflection* of your earthly dad. He is the *perfection* of your earthly dad.

God's not just a bigger version of your earthly father. He's everything you've ever wanted your dad to be and more.

This is great news for us all! Even if your dad is a really wonderful father, you still don't want him to be your God, and you don't want God to be exactly like him. You want a God who is somewhat like him but infinitely better. And that's what you have.

And if you've been trying to overcome the wounds of a terrible earthly dad, and you're thinking you'll never be able to relate to God as a father because you don't even know how, I encourage you to think again. Even if your dad left a wake of pain and confusion and weakened you more than he helped make you strong, you can still imagine what it would have been like if things had been different.

It's likely you *have* imagined what life would be like with a loving, engaged, encouraging, interested dad. What if your earthly father *did* sit patiently on the end of your bed and ask you to tell him all about your day? Haven't you imagined what his embrace would have felt like? What it would have been like if he put the newspaper down or turned the volume down on the television remote and noticed you? Didn't you wonder how things would have been different if he had shown up and sobered up and stayed true and defended you? Haven't you tried to imagine your dad being like this?

God is not the *reflection* of your earthly dad.

He is the *perfection* of your earthly dad.

The good news is that God is what you've imagined all these years. He's everything you've always wanted and so much more! You can use those longings and desires to find your way to Him, knowing that He's not an oversize version of your dad; He's the perfect Father you have always dreamed of. From the pages of Scripture you can know that . . .

- You are the apple of His eye.
- He saw you long before you saw Him.
- You are His unique and purposed creation.
- You have been loved by Him since before there was time.
- He sought you and paid a ransom for you before you did one thing to deserve it.
- He never gave up on you.
- Before God ever asked anything from you, He gave everything to you in the gift of His Son.
- You matter to God.
- You have a destiny.
- You are a somebody.
- You have God-given gifts.
- You are not the center of all creation, but you are dearly loved by the One who is!
- You have access to the throne of grace.
- You have a seat at the table of heaven.
- You have a God to call Father.
- And you have a God who calls you daughter. Son.

Your Father in heaven is a Healer. He can heal all the wounds your earthly father may have caused you. He can pick you up and hold you in His care. He can redeem what has been lost and make all things new again. His arms are strong and His heart is good and you can trust Him.

But how?

Facing the Woundedness

The Enemy is constantly whispering in your ear: "Hey, you can't trust God, because remember what your dad did to you? Remember how your dad broke your heart? Sooner or later, God's going to do the same thing."

How do you get past this hurdle? How do you silence the voice of the Enemy that's ringing in your head and causing you to lock your heart in a vault, never to be wounded again?

First you have to take serious stock of your pain. I don't believe, as some do, that the driving factor in all our lives are our "father wounds." I don't believe every person has been broken by their earthly dad. Yet father wounds are real, and for some, these places of hurt are the dominating factor shaping how they view themselves and how they relate to others. Talking with many people as a pastor, it is staggering how many of their struggles are connected to their relationship (or lack thereof) with their father.

If this describes you, then the first step toward freedom is to face up to the pain and hurt. Ignoring our wounds isn't going to help them heal. Acting like we're fine or setting out to prove that we don't care about what our father did to us is not realistic and will only keep us stuck in the past.

When I was about ten years old, my dad spent six months working in Holland. When he arrived back in Atlanta, he came bearing gifts for my mom, my sister, and me. I'll never forget the moment he handed me a little box containing a red Swiss Army knife. Score! Though only four inches long, this contraption had a dozen different apparatuses on it: among them a corkscrew, tiny scissors, a nail file, a toothpick, and several different knife blades. Granted, my dad probably picked it up at the airport, but I was too young to care or let that chill my mood. This thing was legit, and my mom's disapproval only made me love it more. Dad gave me a quick tutorial, highlighted by the instruction to always use the knife blade in a motion away from my body. "Always cut away from you," he warned. "Understand?"

"Yes, Dad, I get it. Always cut like this," I said, as I motioned with the knife away from myself.

A few weeks later, while Mom and Dad had guests over for dinner and a game of cards, I locked myself in my parents' bathroom and proceeded to hone my carving skills (which were none) on a foot-long piece of 4 x 4 wood that was left over from the stereo cabinet Dad was building. Perched on the toilet, I grabbed the wood in one hand and started whittling away with the large, three-inch blade. About five minutes into the process, the inevitable happened. Foolishly, I was carving the wood toward my body when the blade slipped and sliced into my left hand. The blade sped right through that patch of skin that forms the webbing between your thumb and index finger. I'll spare further description for the sake of the faint of heart, but suffice it to say, blood went everywhere. I didn't want to interrupt the card game, but this couldn't wait.

"Mom, I hurt my hand real bad," I confessed as I sheepishly said hi to our guests. Turning my back to the table, I pulled back the red wad of toilet paper that I was pressing into the wound.

Her eyes widened.

"How did you do that?" she asked.

"I was carving with my new knife Dad got me and it slipped."

"Well, we'll look at it after our company is gone," she said. "And try not to get blood on the carpet."

This was a classic response from my mom. Though dramatic at times, she always underreacted when I hurt myself. After their friends went home, she surveyed the cut, ran some water over it in the bathroom sink, and patched it up with Band-Aids and gauze. That night I got a lecture from Dad (prompted by Mom), and the Swiss Army knife was confiscated as punishment for violating rule "numero uno."

Fifty years later the scar on my left hand confirms the knife wound left a two-inch opening, which rendered my hand pretty much useless for some time. It was a stitches-requiring gash, for sure. But instead of an emergency room visit, we just covered it as best we could, and I tried not to move my thumb for a week or so.

Sadly, things did not improve. Days went by and the bandages were changed, but the wound looked worse and worse, becoming infected and gross. I never did get stitches, and somehow my hand eventually healed, but I can tell you that trying to ignore a wound by covering it up is not the recommended course of action.

The same is true of the wounds to our hearts. We cannot simply ignore the sting of a father's wounds. Sometimes we try by thinking things like:

- *I don't care about my dad. I couldn't care less what he did or didn't do.*
- *I don't need him anyway.*
- *I'm fine, and I'll never let him know how much he hurt me.*
- *What he did then has nothing to do with me now.*
- *I'm better off without him.*
- *If that's the way he feels about me, then that's the way I'll feel about him.*
- *My dad is a loser and I'll never be like him.*
- *I don't care if I ever see him again.*
- *My future husband will be so much better than my dad.*

But such statements only reinforce one thing: your disappointment with your dad and the way his actions have impacted your life. Notice that the common denominator in every phrase are the words "he" and "him." You can't get past the wounds of your dad by repeatedly insisting that you're not impacted by the wounds inflicted by him. And you can't say you don't need your earthly dad's blessing without admitting there is a blessing that you are living without.

So how do we uncover the wounds and find healing for our souls?

To get past our wounds we have to first stare them in the face and admit how they have made us feel. We have to acknowledge the truth of our pain. We have to rip off the Band-Aid and get in touch with the reality that's underneath. We can't afford to ignore the wounds. But we can't stay in the past either—always pushing on our wounds, always probing with questions of *why?* They'll never heal that way. So we must shift our focus, understanding that healing doesn't come by ignoring our wounds, but it also will never happen if we fixate on them. Healing comes as we consider another's wounds—namely, the wounds of Jesus.

The path to healing is found in focusing on Jesus' wounds. "He was pierced for our transgressions, he was crushed for our iniquities; the punishment that brought us peace was on him, and by his wounds we are healed" (Isaiah 53:5).

To delve deeper and deeper into your past without a firm grasp of the cross and the victory Jesus won for you there is like attempting to perform open-heart surgery on yourself. If you're in need of a heart transplant, you first must be willing to face it, to admit it. But you also need a heart surgeon, someone who can do for you what you cannot do for yourself.

Wounds are real, and ignoring them can be fatal. But the Heart Surgeon is here, and His name is Jesus.

Let that sink into your soul—healing is here now in the person of Jesus.

Reflect on the Wounds of Christ

I want to close this chapter here—with the solution within range, but the solution not spelled out for us yet. I want to let us just sit with this tension that we might feel as we think about our earthly fathers.

I know for some of us, that is a difficult place to be, and I want to respect the slow pace that might be required for us to move on from this place. Just let yourself breathe here. Let your eyes gradually be opened to the wounds of the One who ultimately heals us.

Through our faith in Christ, we can all find healing, and we can all find the Father we have been longing for all along. And through Christ you *do* have this perfect Father God.

You do.

You do!

My encouragement is for you to ease yourself from one image to the next—from the broken image left by an earthly father to the perfect Father who is drawing near. Respect the time this can take, sure. But also let yourself come alive to this glorious truth. God, your Abba, has gone to extraordinary lengths to let you know how much you matter to Him—and we'll take a closer look at that next.

Chapter 5

The Tale of Two Trees

Fatherhood is central to the story of God.

We see this in the connection between the last words of the first section of Scripture (what we call the Old Testament) and the first words of the section that begins with the story of Jesus' birth (the New Testament).

As the Old Testament comes to a close, God's people were stuck in their stubborn, sinful ways. God's love and grace and leadership were constantly available to them, but more often than not they chose to go it alone, figuring things out in their own wisdom. They had mostly left behind their idols by this point, but they were not honoring the ways of God or trusting in His faithful character. They were stingy in their gifts toward God's house of worship and dishonest in their dealing with Him, as if He didn't fully know their hearts.

Everything was a mess, yet God still had a redemption plan. In spite of their rebellion, God still loved His people and wanted the best for them. But apparently God was through with their rebuffs. His people weren't listening, and God stopped talking. Between the end of the Old Testament and the beginning of the New Testament, there are four hundred years of history with no recorded message from God.

When we take a copy of Scripture in our hands, it only takes the turn of a page to move from the prophecy of Malachi to Matthew's gospel. Yet that single page turn represents four centuries of silence. Four hundred years where there was no prophet. No promise. Nothing.

But have you ever noticed what the last words of the Old Testament recorded in Scripture are? What message did God leave with His people right before He went silent for four centuries?

> "See, I will send the prophet Elijah to you before that great and dreadful day of the LORD comes. *He will turn the hearts of the parents to their children,* and the hearts of the children to their parents; or else I will come and strike the land with total destruction" (Malachi 4:5–6, emphasis added).

How incredible! The Old Testament ends with a promise underscoring God's desire to restore fatherhood, making right the relationships between children and their fathers. He wants to reconnect the hearts of fathers to their children and reposition children under the waterfall of their father's blessing.

In the broader sense, God is seeking to reestablish His future people in a right understanding of Himself and His ways. Yet in a more specific sense God wants us to realize that

He is working (even through the silence) to make it possible for us to know Him as *Abba Father*.

In these closing words from Malachi, we see both a promise and a cause for us to pause. The promise is that God is *not* going to experience a work stoppage just because the people stopped listening to Him. His plans will remain on track. His mission will not be thwarted.

But we also see a warning in these words. God is assuring us that our rebellion will not go unchecked forever. He wants us to know that the wrath of a holy God is coming. Yet don't miss this—God is merciful and kind. The fiery justice of His righteousness doesn't have to be our end.

How do we know God is merciful and kind? After four hundred years of nothing, the lingering silence of heaven was broken by the cry of a baby in Bethlehem, because this is what God had to say next . . .

God Starts Talking Again

Imagine how eager the angel was who got the assignment to declare to the shepherds that a Savior had been born nearby during the night. For centuries there had been no messenger, but now the announcement that would change history was made: "A Savior has been born to you; he is the Messiah, the Lord" (Luke 2:11).

Actually, a few angel visits had taken place in the months leading up to Jesus' birth. The angel Gabriel appeared to a man named Zechariah promising the birth of John the Baptist. The angel told Zechariah that his son, John, would have a favored role in the story of God. John was going to prepare the way for Jesus by calling people to change their ways and turn to the Lord. And he was also going to do something else:

And he will go on before the Lord, in the spirit and power of Elijah, *to turn the hearts of the parents to their children* and the disobedient to the wisdom of the righteous—to make ready a people prepared for the Lord. (Luke 1:17, emphasis added)

We see that through John, God was fulfilling the last words of the Old Testament.

In the first chapter of the New Testament, God is shown keeping His promise and preparing a way for the hearts of fathers to change, making a way to restore the relationship between fathers and children. Making a way for your heart to change and a way to bring healing between you and your earthly father. Why? Because fatherhood matters to God. It matters so much because ultimately, He's making a way to bring healing between you and your heavenly Father.

Malachi's prophetic words come true as Jesus comes to earth, God in human skin. Jesus didn't just come to do some good works and heal those with diseases. He wasn't on earth just to walk on water and raise His buddy Lazarus from the dead. Jesus came to die, to do what no other person ever born could do. Born of a virgin and without sin, Jesus lived obedient to the Father so that He could exchange His innocent life for yours. In so doing, He canceled your debt of sin and death and offered you the gift of never-ending life.

This is the glorious gospel story that fuels this book and everything else about the Christian message. And this heavenly exchange offers you a fatherhood possibility that is almost beyond comprehension. You may be thinking, *I appreciate that Jesus gave His life so I could be forgiven and have peace with God, but what does that have to do with what happened between me and my dad?* Sometimes we get all tangled up in our family tree, and we fail to see the primacy of the tree that is the cross of Calvary and the vital connection between the two.

Think of it this way: Jesus willingly took on all the wrong of every one of us on the cross. That means God transferred all of our wrong—and all of your dad's wrong—onto the blameless life of His Son. Once that happened, Jesus bore the guilt of our sinful ways, and thus He bore the weight of God's wrath that we deserved. Remember that Scripture says Jesus was "pierced for our transgressions, he was crushed for our iniquities" (Isaiah 53:5).

The significance of the baby's birth, which broke centuries of silence, that I want you to see is this: When Jesus chose to die on that cross, He was forsaken by His Father so that you would never have to live a day without a father's blessing. He was forsaken by His heavenly Father so that you would never have to be forsaken by God. Jesus accomplished the work on the cross to give you a new family tree.

And this new family tree changes everything.

Never Left Behind

As the wrath of God fell on Jesus, the sky turned black and an earthquake shook the ground. Then moments from death Jesus cried out, "My God, my God, why have you forsaken me?" (Matthew 27:46).

What staggering words to come from the lips of this Son who had lived for thirty-three years on earth (and for all of eternity past) in an inseparable bond with His Father. Yet now, covered with our shame, Jesus knew what it was to be forsaken by His almighty Father.

Abandoned.
Naked.
Beaten.
Humiliated.
Alone.
Wounded.
Rejected.

That's how Jesus died. When He died, Jesus made good on the hope set forth in Malachi's last prophetic bridge to the future. Now, through Christ, God could forgive you. Cover your sins, cancel your debt, and cast away your shame forever. Raise you with Christ to new life and call you son or daughter. Jesus was forsaken so that you would never have to live a day without a father's blessing!

Dive deep into this truth! Because of what Jesus has done

Jesus was forsaken
so that you would

**never
have to
live a day
without
a father's
blessing!**

for you, you can be born again through faith in Him into the family of God and always have access to the Father's blessing. When you are in God's family, you will never be forgotten.

Jesus took on Himself every curse that is over your life, especially the curse of living without a father's love, acceptance, and approval. Jesus did this when He was hoisted up on Calvary's tree, as it is written with reference to the cross, "Cursed is everyone who is hung on a tree" (Galatians 3:13 NLT). And because of Christ's work, this is your new identity:

- Jesus was cursed so that you could be cured.
- Jesus was rejected so that you could be accepted.
- Jesus experienced the wrath of God's righteous judgment so that you could be released from the weight of sin and shame.
- Jesus was broken on the cross so that your shattered destiny could be put back together again.
- Jesus became sin so that you could become the righteousness of God in Him.
- Jesus was wounded so you could be healed.

Once your eyes are opened to the transforming power of Jesus' death, you understand that the cross is not just an important moment in the annals of history; the cross is the place where your reason for existence is defined. It's the place where you can step into your purpose as you claim God's forgiveness and fatherhood. As your relationship with God is changed, you find that human relationships can change too, and by the same means. If you want to go forward toward healing in your relationship with your earthly dad, you must return to the cross of Christ again and again. It's the place where you were no longer orphaned, no matter your past.

And you must see the cross through eyes opened by the Spirit of God.

A Glimpse of the Cross

One night on a college retreat with my church on St. Simons Island, Georgia, I had a revelation that shifted the trajectory of my life. I was sitting with some friends on the last row in the auditorium as our pastor, Dr. Charles Stanley, was teaching on abiding in Christ from John's gospel. Everything was pretty normal until the response time as he was praying over the group at the end of his message. Suddenly all the extraneous thoughts vanished from my mind's eye, and all I could see was Jesus hanging on the cross. I didn't visibly see the cross, and I don't know what Jesus physically looked like hanging there. But I saw an image of Jesus on the cross, bloody and battered, a ring of thorns pressed into His head and agony on His face.

I was a church kid. I'd heard about the cross all my life and believed in its power to save. I sang about it, taught Bible studies on it, read about it. But in that moment, everything changed. *I had a revelation of the cross.*

What stopped me in my mental tracks was the realization that it was *my* cross. Jesus was hanging on a cross that I should have been on. It was my sin, my guilt, my wrong that put Him there. And He was taking all the punishment I deserved so I could go free.

Dr. Stanley ended his prayer, and everyone headed for another building where the big event of the night was to build your own banana split. Many ice cream flavors would be laid out with all the toppings imaginable, and you'd get to make yours just the way you wanted it. (Yes, this was a big draw for church retreats back in the day.) But suddenly I couldn't care less about dessert or seeing the girl I was interested in or laughing with my friends. I mumbled to them to go on without me and I sat there frozen in my newfound revelation. I couldn't move out of my chair.

That night God opened the eyes of my heart.

Similarly, God doesn't just want you to know about the cross. He wants you to see it in such a way that it shakes you to the core and awakens you to an eye-opening realization that can alter the direction of your life. That's the kind of unveiling He wants to give you, a revelation that allows you to be changed in an instant. It happened to one of the soldiers who nailed Jesus to that beam of wood. Just moments after Jesus breathed His last breath, the centurion declared, "Surely this man was the Son of God!" (Mark 15:39). He had heard people say all kinds of things about Jesus, about who He claimed to be. But in those moments watching Jesus die, the centurion received spiritual sight and he *knew for himself* exactly who Jesus was.

We can't just breeze past the cross. It's important for us to see that something powerful and gruesome and gutsy happened there. As awful as Jesus' death was for Him, it's the best thing that ever happened to you and me. Once we truly see it, we are free. We see it and confess, *I am forgiven!*

Radical grace invades our story. Guilt and condemnation are sent packing. We realize that through faith in Jesus we are made new—we get a fresh start. This new beginning is not about something we do; it's about someone we believe in and, as a result, someone we become. We are born again as sons and daughters of a perfect Father. But that's not the end of the story. Something else happens. As we begin to realize that we are the recipients of the most amazing grace, it starts dawning on us that we have the ability to reflect that same powerful grace to others.

And that includes your dad.

But before you can go forward in making peace with your dad, you have to first go back to the place where your heavenly Father made peace with you.

In this process, you can be completely honest about your feelings about what happened with your dad. Maybe your father divorced your mom and left the family when you were young. Or perhaps he died of cancer or a heart attack or some other disease. Or maybe he broke your trust and your heart and, as a result, put you and your family through a roller coaster ride of highs and lows, with some promises kept but a lot more broken. Or maybe your dad hurt you, robbed your innocence, beat you, cursed you, or told you he wished you'd never been born. Or maybe there's no father to reconcile things with. Your dad split long before you were born, or worse, he doesn't even know you're alive on planet Earth. If he did, would he come to find you? Would he care? Would he love you? Would he be proud of you?

What do you do with all the pain and brokenness that you've experienced because of your earthly dad? Where was this *perfect heavenly Father* when all this was happening? And if the *perfect Father* is so good and loves you so much, then why didn't He stop things or change the situation?

To be honest, there aren't simple answers to these questions. There's no one-size-fits-all bandage that can make sense of your hurt and pain. But there is a history-shaping cross standing in the middle of your story.

As I sit with people and am invited into their pain, I always seek to help them focus on the cross of Jesus. It's real. And immovable. And gritty. And glorious. And it's the only place we can find healing in the midst of deep, heart-shattering pain. It's where you need to camp if you have a life story blown apart by the actions of your earthly dad, because the place you find peace with your heavenly Father is the same place you're going to find the possibility of peace with your earthly dad. Peace is found in the cross of Christ.

As your eyes are opened to see the cross, several key truths about the work Jesus did on the cross will help sustain you in the darkest times, and I encourage you to meditate on these:

1. The cross of Christ will reinforce that God loves you.

The Enemy is already telling you that if God loved you, then these terrible, painful things wouldn't have occurred.

Obviously God doesn't love you, Satan drones. *If He did love you then why would all these horrible things be happening to you?*

Soon, we start repeating Satan's lies to ourselves and others.

We think, *There's something wrong with me. Or maybe God is trying to punish me. Or maybe He just doesn't care. Or maybe He isn't even there.*

But the cross is indisputable proof that God loves you because it's the place where He gave His best for you.

You may be thinking, *I don't feel loved.* Fortunately, the love God displayed for you doesn't begin with a feeling. His love is demonstrated in a reality. Jesus *really* died for you. So we start by believing a reality, sinking our thoughts into the truth of what happened on the cross. In time our feelings will follow as we remind ourselves again and again of what happened there.

This is love: not that we loved God, but that he loved us and sent his Son as an atoning sacrifice for our sins. (1 John 4:10)

But God demonstrates his own love for us in this: While we were still sinners, Christ died for us. (Romans 5:8)

2. The cross of Christ is the place that allows you to know that God understands your pain.

Your heavenly Father knows what it's like to watch His Son suffer and die. And Jesus knows the depths of anguish just like you. Jesus is not indifferent to your pain. He understands what you are feeling and has been crushed by the darkness.

A few years back, during a Q&A before one of our Passion Worship Night tour stops, an interesting question came from a young girl in the crowd. Her question was one we'd never gotten before. In a pre-event format like this one, the questions usually range from "How'd you guys get your start in ministry?" to "How do you stay balanced with church, tour, speaking, and all the other things you have going?"

When her turn came, she said, "I've experienced a murder in my family, and I don't know what to do. Can God help someone like me?"

What do you say in a moment like that, especially when the question catches you off guard?

After a pause, I told her first how sorry I was to know that she had walked through something so difficult, living with the lingering reality that life was snatched away from someone in her family. I also told her I couldn't fully relate to her situation because I hadn't experienced anything like it, but I knew God could. God could relate fully.

And then the Spirit helped me. While I was answering her I was reminded that God has witnessed a murder in His family too. He watched as evil men took the life of His Son (yes, it was His plan, but it was carried out by hate-filled men). I had never spoken of Christ's death in those terms before, but I had never been asked that question before either. God understands her pain and yours. How do you know? The cross of Christ is proof.

3. The cross of Christ is proof that God can take the worst and bring something good from it.

I know that can sound trite, like a church soundbite. And it would be if the cross of Jesus wasn't in your story, casting such a powerful legacy of hope over your life.

Let's be honest. If we had been eyewitnesses to the death

of Jesus, we would be convinced that we'd been privy to the worst this sinful world has to offer. "What an awful day," we'd say. "Could anything ever be worse than today?"

The innocent Son of God was unjustly killed via one of the most excruciating means of execution ever devised. Even earth couldn't watch as darkness shrouded the cross in the middle of the afternoon.

But three days later Jesus beat death, overcoming sin, hell, and the grave. By the power of God, Jesus was alive again, victorious and free. Today, after more than two thousand years of history have passed, us followers of Jesus don't call that day "Bad Friday." No; it's the opposite. We call it "Good Friday." We don't claim it as the worst day in history; we sing about it as the best thing that ever happened to the human race. Why? Because God took the worst and turned it into the best.

Facing Your Family Tree

If God can bring about our best from Christ's worst, He can surely overcome the mangled web of destruction left by people in your life. God can restore and bring about something beautiful from the chaos in your life, the legacy of devastation in your past. He can and will bring the change that displays His power and love. Oh, and this is not some fairytale promise I'm offering or some wishful mumbo jumbo. It's bedrock truth anchored in history at the cross of Jesus.

The prophet Joel proclaimed that God says, "I will repay

you for the years the locusts have eaten" (Joel 2:25). So even if the sin of your father, or his foolishness or disinterest or failure, has left your heart like a devastated mountainside, clear-cut of everything beautiful and fruitful and promising, it's not the end of your story. Even if a firestorm of destruction has left your life bare, God is in the business of giving beauty for ashes, and that's what He wants to do for you.

The Enemy is trying to drive a wedge between you and God by using what has happened with your dad to make you doubt that God's heart is good and His arms are strong. Yet a new understanding and a fresh glimpse of the finished work of the cross can forge a bond between you and your heavenly Father that cannot be broken.

Calvary's tree is always primary over anyone's earthly family tree. On Calvary's tree Jesus made a way for you to join a new family as a forgiven son or daughter of the King. Through Jesus you are now a part of the best family of all. But He's placed you in your particular human family for a reason.

In the next chapter we'll look more closely at how your powerful new identity as God's child changes you and how it can transform your earthly family tree with that same miracle power.

Chapter 6

Reverse the Curse

For the past few years it has become more and more popular for people to want to know about their ancestry. To know where they came from. Advances in technology make it more accessible and affordable than ever before. All you have to do is pay a company for its services, and soon, a collection kit arrives at your front door. You gather a dollop of saliva and ship it back in the enclosed package. That's it. A few weeks later, you receive access to your data telling you all about your people, your origin.

I know a lot of people have received their results, and it's fascinating. The info breaks down your origin by percentage and region of the world. For example, yours might tell you that your origin is 43 percent East African, 23 percent Southern European, 11 percent Western European, and 2 percent Native American. For good measure, there's usually 1 percent "unidentified" in the mix. All that from a blob of spit!

I haven't gone through the process, but if I do, I'm really

hoping it will confirm that I have substantial Italian (Sicilian) and Greek roots! Hey, with a name like Louie Giglio, what else would you expect?

My point is there's a growing fascination with origin. Who am I? Where did I come from? What does my family tree really look like? Do I have branches in the Middle East? Asia? Africa?

Here's a headline for you: Because Christ hung on that God-forsaken tree of the cross, you are invited to become part of a brand-new family tree. Yep. You still have to navigate your earthly family tree, but you can be born into a new family by faith in Jesus.

The Gift of a New Family Tree

The most apt description of what it means to be spiritually saved is the phrase *born again*. Granted, it was more prevalent to hear that phrase from people coming out of the Jesus Movement in the 1960s and from the preaching of Billy Graham. And from the words of former president Jimmy Carter as he introduced the phrase to broader culture in the 1970s, announcing to the world that he was "a born-again Christian."

Yet the term *born again* is not simply a mantra of Christian leaders. This is a revolutionary teaching of Jesus Himself. When asked by a Jewish religious leader how he could make his way into the kingdom of God, Jesus answered, "You must be born again." Nicodemus, the man who asked Jesus the question, was baffled. "How can I be born again now that I am a fully grown man? I can't enter my mom's womb a second time!"

For sure, a second physical birth was a crazy idea. But Jesus was talking about spiritual birth. He was pointing out the problem of sin (that it makes us spiritually dead) and the hope embraced by the good news (that Jesus came to give spiritual life). That's why Jesus said "you must be born a second time." Not born of the flesh but of the *Spirit*.

We don't get into God's family by being good enough or trying our best. And we don't get left out of His family because we've been bad or we don't think we deserve His love. God is an equal opportunity heavenly Father who has created each of us in His image and who loved us enough to give His Son so that each of us could be born again to brand-new, never-ending life!

Galatians 4:4–7 describes this same mind-boggling truth. The summary of it is that God sent His Son to redeem people from a broken planet Earth so that these people would become His children. Fully adopted. Fully new. Fully alive. Full sons and daughters of a good and perfect Father.

There is a catch. You must receive His gift. You must confess that you have fallen short of God's best and accept the forgiveness the Father offers through the cross. When you do, Scripture says everything changes. The Spirit of God enters your life and brings your spirit to life. This new birth doesn't simply place you on the membership roll of the church or tip the scales of your bad deeds a little toward the good side. This new birth firmly grafts you into God's family tree as a son or daughter.

Let that settle into your soul.

Remember, God is on a mission to restore the hearts of the fathers to their children and the hearts of the children toward their fathers. This mission doesn't start by fixing the issues in your human family tree. The process starts by God placing you into a new family, into a new relationship with Him.

If you were to draw out your earthly family tree, what would it look like? For some of you it would look pretty straightforward. Two sets of grandparents, Mom and Dad, me and my two sisters. Yeah, a few cousins and aunts and uncles— pretty simple. But others might need more paper to add in stepparents, half-siblings, or extra sets of step-grandparents. You might puzzle over what to do with names of people you're technically still related to but who are no longer on the scene. You might need an eraser to correct your mistakes before figuring it all out.

Your family tree may look beautiful, with a solid trunk and healthy leaves. Or it may be bent by stormy winds, with cracked branches and fading leaves. Whatever it looks like, you're stuck with it. That earthly family tree is a nonnegotiable for you.

But that's not where your story ends. Thanks to Christ, you can be placed in a new tree. God the heavenly Father has given you new life through God the Son by the work of God the Spirit. A triune God—Father, Son, and Spirit—is at the head of your tree, and you are a direct descendant!

You're not some third cousin twice removed who is barely sneaking into the kingdom of God with everyone looking across heaven's living room saying, "Who is that? How'd they get in here? Are we related?"

No, if you are born again in Christ, you can take a swab of your spiritual DNA and send it through the test of the Holy Spirit and the Word. You'll get results back that will blow you away. We'll dive more into the new you in later chapters, but suffice it to say the paternity test of heaven will come back positive. In Christ, your heavenly Father has brought you to life, and you are His.

Just as He gave you life at your physical birth—God conceiving you in your mother's womb and knitting you together to His exact specifications—God the Father gave you your first spiritual breath when you were born again. His name is on your spiritual birth certificate. And He promises to be your Father every step of the way until you are with Him in heaven. What an awesome privilege to be called a child of the King.

This is a game-changing reality. Even if there was little or no father's blessing for you that came down your earthly family tree, you still have a better Father's blessing coming down your new family tree. Right now, you are standing under the waterfall of the Father-blessing of God.

Way Bigger Than Niagara

The waterfall of God's fatherly blessing is not like one of those thin, ribbon-like waterfalls you see on the side of the road while driving through the foothills. It's more like Niagara Falls, or the great Victoria Falls on the border between Zambia and Zimbabwe. His love is a like a torrent, relentless and unending, unconditional and pure, gently roaring His blessing over your life. And His love is pouring down on you right now.

If you close your eyes for a moment, can you picture it? Can you see yourself standing under a steady flow of love, smiling in the crashing foam of a perfect Father's blessing? In Christ, that's exactly where you are. Here are some incredible facts about this blessing:

- You will always have enough of His blessing.
  (2 Corinthians 9:8)
- You will never exhaust His love. (Jeremiah 31:3)
- You will never fully deplete His goodness. (Psalm 23:6)
- Every single day His mercy will awaken you.
  (Lamentations 3:22–23)

This reality, this constant waterfall of blessing, will fill you, heal you, and transform your wounded heart into a heart that's new. And it's going to do something else miraculous. This perfect Father's blessing is going to allow you to reverse whatever curse has fallen on you.

This perfect Father's blessing
is going to allow you to

reverse whatever curse has fallen on you.

You are no longer going to live in such a way that you're defined as "forgotten." From now on you are called beloved daughter. Beloved son. You will no longer face life from a deficit. You will face life with a sense of adequacy, knowing you have an abundant waterfall above you, the blessing constantly filling you with all you need.

Your life is not going to be likened to a run-on sentence of "what ifs" and "buts" and "only ifs." You are going to know that you belong to the God of the universe and that nothing can thwart His purpose and plans for your life. You are going to discover new power inside, the very power of the Spirit of God. And your eyes are going to be opened to understand that God's power can do the one thing that for now seems impossible for you to do. Standing under this mind-blowing blessing, grafted into a new family tree, you are going to find the power to forgive your earthly dad for all the hurt and wrong and pain he brought into your life.

I get that this step may take some time. But I don't buy into the thinking that it's not possible for you to forgive your dad.

You may be thinking, *Louie, I was with you up to this point, but you simply don't understand what I've been through. There's no way I'm ever forgiving my dad after what he did to me.*

That kind of thinking reflects the *old you*, the one who was left behind, bruised, ignored, abused. There is a *new you* on the scene. A loved and blessed and approved and accepted you—a new you who has a new name and a new family tree and a new Spirit within you.

Think about it this way:

- If God can overwhelm the grave and rise from the dead,
- If He can cancel the debt of sin you owe,
- If He can make peace between you and a holy God,
- If He has the power to free you from death and raise you up to eternal life,
- If He can re-create you by the Spirit and make you a child . . .

. . . then He can certainly give you power over your past. Jesus can be in and through you a curse-breaking force for your life and for the generations to come after you.

It all begins with a supernatural word—*forgiveness*.

The Power of Forgiveness

That's where your new story begins. Even Jesus said it from the cross about those who were hurling insults at Him. Looking at the very ones who drove the nails into His hands and feet, He said, "Father, forgive them, for they do not know what they are doing" (Luke 23:34).

And He's spoken it to you, even though when you pushed back on His truth and ignored His love you *did* know what you were doing. The trajectory of your eternity began to change the moment you opened the door to God telling you that He forgives you. In the same way, when you've received God's forgiveness, your healing finds its fullness when you allow God to help you reflect His forgiveness to those around you.

But, Louie, my dad doesn't deserve to be forgiven. My dad has never once even acknowledged his wrong. My dad wouldn't even care if I wanted to forgive him. There's no way. I don't see that happening—me forgiving him. I'm willing to move on, but to forgive what he did to me, I don't think I can do that.

First, it's important to emphasize that when I say to forgive, I'm not suggesting that you sweep the past under the rug. That you simply act like abuse or betrayal or abandonment didn't happen or excuse it. No way! Forgiveness is not a *free pass* for the person who has wounded you. And forgiveness doesn't mean that you might not require boundaries in your relationship with your earthly father going forward. The forgiveness I'm encouraging you toward is rooted in Christ's love and justice.

Also, just so we're clear right up front, I'm not encouraging you to continue to put yourself in harm's way or refuse to shine the light of accountability where needed if that's the case. No, forgiveness is not turning a blind eye to wrong. God didn't do that with our wrongs. He leveled them squarely onto the innocent life of His Son and punished our sinfulness to the full extent of the law. When God offers forgiveness, He's not ignoring our shortcomings and rebellious ways. God is offering a Son He had to turn away from in His last moments on the cross and extending to us grace we did not deserve.

To forgive your dad is not to release him *from* the consequences of his actions; rather it's to release him *to God* who has said, "Vengeance is mine . . . says the Lord" (Romans 12:19 ESV). You don't release your dad *from something* as much as you release him *to someone.* You offload the role of being judge and jury to God, who is just and fair, knowing full well that your heavenly Father will exact justice at the right time and in the right way.

Bitterness continues to pave a path to your past while forgiveness paves a way to your future. Trust me, your dad won't get off the hook with God. But by extending forgiveness, you can get off the hook of resentment and anger that's been keeping your life stuck in reverse.

Your dad may not want forgiveness or even think he needs it. He might reject your efforts at making peace and never answer your offer of grace. He may never take your call. He may never admit his wrong. He may even be dead and gone. But the power forgiveness can bring to you does not happen when and if your dad receives it. The power of forgiveness breaks your chains the moment you offer it.

You may still be thinking, *Why on earth would I want to do that?*

I get it. It's a big deal to let go of something you've been carrying for a long time. But, in Christ, God wants you to see yourself in a completely new way. God wants to bring you out of that state of mind where you see yourself with less— that's the you who was left to fend for yourself while your dad was busy being an addict or a workaholic or "finding himself." God invites you to have a new set of eyes with a new vision of yourself taking your seat at His royal table. You now have the blessing of a perfect Father—and the position, and the forgiveness, and the power of the Spirit that comes with being His.

Your life is no longer dictated by what was done to you. Your life is defined by what Christ has done for you. You are not a victim but a beloved child sharing in Christ's victory. You're no longer smashed into the ash heap, but you are raised up with Jesus to sit with Him in heaven's heights. You are a child of God. And you are free to rise above the past and do for your dad the same thing your heavenly Father did for you—forgive.

The Poison of Unforgiveness

In the end you may choose not to forgive. That's your decision. But before making that choice, please consider the deceptive nature of unforgiveness. To not forgive gives us a false sense of control. We think, *My dad did all this to me, and I had no say in that. But I've got control now and I can decide how I want to treat him.* By hanging on to our urge for revenge, we think we've got the upper hand.

But is this really true? Or is it possible that the Enemy has duped us into a faulty way of thinking? He wants us to think that by not forgiving, *we* hold the power. Yet any time we refuse to forgive, we continue to give power to the past.

Think about it: You could be stuck in the past with a root of bitterness eating a hole in your soul while your dad is on a hunting trip in the mountains with his buddies, oblivious to the fact that you're *not forgiving* him again today. He's not even seeking reconciliation.

If we refuse to extend forgiveness to our fathers, that action doesn't punish our dads. Rather, it imprisons us. It anchors us to the negative while God wants to move us into the fullness of who our heavenly Father is and who He says we are in Him. It's impossible to fully experience all God has for us while we are holding on with clenched fists to the past.

So I gently ask: Is your refusal to forgive your dad bringing you more peace or more pain? Is it helping you move forward or is it always pulling you back into the past? Has unwillingness to forgive led you to the freedom you hoped it would, or is it unsettling to your heart?

If the answers are all negative, then please know that God desires to give you the "revelation sight" we talked about before—a great conjunction of understanding that you are a loved child of a perfect Father. This is sight not just to see God as a perfect Father but to see the cross of Christ and the resulting power you can now access through the Spirit within you. The passage we noted goes on to say this:

> I pray that the eyes of your heart may be enlightened in order that you may know the hope to which he has called you, the riches of his glorious inheritance in his holy people, and *his incomparably great power for us who believe.*

That power is the same as the mighty strength he exerted when he raised Christ from the dead and seated him at his right hand in the heavenly realms, far above all rule and authority, power and dominion, and every name that is invoked, not only in the present age but also in the one to come. (Ephesians 1:18–21, emphasis added)

God wants you to see that you have true power through Him. Power not to tightly grip the past, to hold out and never forgive. It's the opposite—God is giving you the power to let go of anger and offer to your dad the grace he doesn't deserve.

Forgiveness is not easy work, and often the seemingly easier route is to try to lock our disappointment and anger away in a closet while we zone out on Xbox, binge another TV series, scroll through social media, dive deeper into raising our kids, amp up our workouts, or invest all our energy in excelling at work. The process of forgiving someone who has deserted us or wronged us is sometimes as painful as the hurt we experienced in the first place.

But this healing is worth the hurt.

Fixing Broken Things

The simple apartment where I grew up was a three-bedroom, two-bath affair in a sprawling complex off a busy road in the suburbs of Atlanta. Each building had four units, and as I mentioned earlier, we lived in building 29 in the downstairs unit on the right. One summer night my friends and I were sitting on the hood of an old-timey car parked at the end of the adjacent building. The car was parked above the retaining wall that rose about three feet higher than the ground, and it had a thin metal bumper that stuck out like an arc. I rested my feet on the bumper as we sat on the hood, and when my dad opened our front door and let out his trademark whistle, it told me it was time to head for home.

My plan was to slide off the hood, spring with both feet off the bumper, leap into the air, and land on the ground. Sadly my right foot slipped and my right leg slid between the bumper and the car. But it was too late to stop my motion, and the rest of me tumbled airborne. What happened next is hard to think about. A loud *crack* rang out and I immediately knew something was wrong.

When I landed on the ground I screamed in agony and grabbed my right leg just below the knee. I knew it was bad and asked a friend to run to my house and get my mom. My mom didn't come, but the friend returned with a message instead.

"Your mom said you better get home right now. If not, you're going to be grounded!"

"Go get my dad," I said, knowing he'd be there in a flash. A few minutes later I was in my dad's arms and headed to the house. He sat me down on the toilet seat in the bathroom while my mom surveyed the huge abrasion on my shin. "I'll put some Mercurochrome on it," she offered, "and we'll keep an eye on it."

"No, mom, it hurts really bad," I insisted.

"Okay, try to stand up and see if you can put your weight on it," she said, while talking on the corded phone to my step-grandmother who worked as a nurse at the local hospital.

My scream was even louder this time as through tears I told my mom I couldn't stand up. As a last resort, my dad loaded me into the car, and we headed to the emergency room at Piedmont Hospital where they x-rayed my leg. The doctor on duty was Dr. James Funk, a renowned orthopedic surgeon in Atlanta at the time and the team doctor for Atlanta's professional sports teams. He quickly assessed the problem—my shin was snapped in two about an inch below my kneecap.

It was clear from his expression that Dr. Funk had a plan in mind.

Poor dad. He didn't do well with watching me or my sister suffer. In fact, I think he was actually puffing on a cigarette in the corner of the examination room. (It was the 1960s, after all.) He was in about as much pain as I was. Dr. Funk announced he'd have to set my leg and put it in a cast. Within a few minutes a nurse appeared with a needle that was long enough to knit with. She proceeded to stab me in the shin while another nurse held me down. Man, did I yell. Dad puffed harder.

Once my leg was numb, one of the nurses grabbed me around the waist while Dr. Funk set my leg bone in place. Oh man. That hurt worse than the needle. I screamed even louder.

By now I had forgotten about the initial crack I heard when I fell off the front of the car. The trauma of trying to stand up in the bathroom for my mom was a distant memory. The pain I felt now was on a whole new level. Satisfied he'd gotten the bone straight, Dr. Funk turned to my dad and said, "He's going to be just fine in a few weeks. We'll get a cast on it and he'll be running again by the end of the summer. Oh, and please, you can't smoke in here!"

The plaster cast stretched from my hip to my toes. I think it weighed more than I did. It had a rubber-stopper type thing attached underneath my foot so I could walk, but I had to twist my leg to the side with every step. A hip-to-toe cast in ninety-five-degree weather. What a fun summer that was!

In time, my leg healed. When they sawed the cast off in Dr. Funk's office, my leg had shriveled to the size of a broomstick. When I walked, I turned my leg to the right like I'd been doing on the rubber thingy for twelve weeks in the cast.

Slowly I regained strength in my leg. In a few months I recovered my confidence in walking and running. By the next summer I was moving as fast as ever.

Repairing wrongs and forgiving wounds is a process something like that—not pain free, but the pain is worth it. Setting broken things right is never a cakewalk. Yet, through Christ, God has set your life at peace with Him, and He is giving you the power to be a peacemaker with those around you—including your dad.

And there's something more. Once God helps you forgive, you can flip the script and bless the father who never blessed you. It starts with receiving—with humbly standing under a waterfall of blessing you didn't earn and can never lose. Soon you are looking at your dad in a new light. Again, you're not excusing the past, but you are seeing him as a son, maybe a broken son who never has known the blessing we all crave. Some of you can see it. You know your father's father and know what kind of world your dad had to endure while he was growing up. You see the gaps and have heard the sharp words. Maybe granddad is the antagonist, or was absent, or abusive.

With new sight and new blessing, you have a greater ability to understand your dad. Maybe your father didn't pass the blessing down the tree because he had no idea how to do that. Or maybe when he lashed out at you, he was trying to work through all the blows that had been inflicted on him. Your job is not to psychoanalyze or counsel or even confront all the demons that might be in your dad's past. Your role is to see him as a human being desperately in need of a father's blessing and to recognize that you can offer *him* the blessing he's never known.

As Scripture encourages, our new way of life is to "bless those who persecute you; bless and do not curse" (Romans 12:14). How do we make the shift and respond in this way? We begin by asking God to help us approach others with compassion, and we constantly take our cues from the way God responded to us on the cross.

Decades later, I sat with my dad in the very same hospital where Dr. Funk had set my broken leg. That's where Dad told me he had never been loved; no one had ever wanted him; and God didn't want him either. That day I saw my father in a way I'd never seen him before. Though my dad was in his sixties, I saw a little boy standing in a doorway watching the people he was counting on most vanish from his sight. I'm sure others were careful not to use the word *abandoned* when they tried to explain why his mom and dad weren't around, but did it matter? When you've been left behind you don't need people to tell you what you already know.

While I was learning to live under the heavenly waterfall of a perfect Father's blessing, my dad had spent his whole life searching for a drop of water in a wasteland of desertion. I had come to understand and enjoy the fact that God loved me with arms outstretched. But my dad only knew the opposite, the sound of footsteps walking away from him. He had been left behind and he felt like there was nothing he could do about it.

When I understood this about my dad, everything shifted for me. I realized I had enough blessing for the both of us. I understood it was my privilege to send the blessing up our earthly family tree. I started to tell my dad how much I loved him, how incredible he was to my sister and me. I'd tell him how much I admired him and how, even though we hadn't shared the common ground of faith—the most important part of my life—we shared the same blood, the same loves, the same sense of humor, and the same name. I loved Louie Giglio #2 so much, and I wanted him to hear me say it— "Dad, you're amazing. I love you!"

A few years later a heart attack took my dad from us. When my sister called to tell me, it was the most crushing pain I have ever felt. I cried for weeks, steamrolled with the memory of all the pain we'd been through. There wasn't going to be a pretty bow on the end of our story. There was only pain, and loss, and death.

I don't know how much of the blessing that my family and I were able to speak over my dad was actually processed, received, and believed. But I will forever be grateful for how his disability allowed me to see him in a whole new light. I am so grateful I had the opportunity to forgive (though I really never held much against him) and to bless him. When my dad died, I wasn't mad at him. I mostly felt sorry for all the pain he'd been through. And I wished I'd spoken even more blessing than I did over him while he was alive. But I spoke enough that I believe he knew how much I loved him and how much God loved him too.

A New Tree Blossoms

I'm convinced that once we're in heaven, we will never regret letting go of wrongs and forgiving others in the same way our Father has forgiven us. We will only regret the bitterness we harbored and the anger we held on to while on earth. When we see the risen Jesus, scars still marking His wrists and side, we will wish we'd trusted Him more to empower us to turn the tide of hate and loss and take our place as agents of a better

Reverse the Curse

kingdom. When we see the mighty throne of God and under-stand fully that all justice rests in His hands, we'll wish we had extended more olive branches of peace to those around us.

For now I simply encourage you to park under the waterfall of a better blessing. Remember from the outset it's a blessing you didn't earn or deserve. It's the blessing of a perfect Father with extravagant love, a Father who has never lost sight of you and will never let you go. He is a perfect Abba who will not leave you powerless but who will make you powerful—powerful enough to extend to others the blessing He is extending to you.

As we conclude this chapter, I invite you to come back to that picture of your earthly family tree. Again, it may be the most awesome family tree of all time. Or maybe your family tree isn't so solid. Maybe the leaves are sparse and discolored. The apples are wormy and some are rotten. The branches are cracked and broken and there's a lot of hurt in your family tree. Here's what I want you to do:

Leave your earthly family tree exactly where it is in your mind. Sure, it will always be a part of your life. To some degree you'll always be working through your family tree, figuring out what was passed along to you, sorting out what's helpful and harmful.

But now, superimpose another family tree on top of your earthly family tree. A new family tree, a heavenly family tree. Lay it right over the old earthly tree. This is the gift that God offers us. This family tree has steady branches and a sure trunk. I invite you to overlay a new and fresh image right on top of the old one. This new tree has two main components, with a straight line connecting the two:

1. God, your heavenly Father
2. and you, child of God

In this new family tree, you are always loved, always accepted, always supported, always hoped for, always championed, always cared for. In this new family tree, your perfect Father God says something like, *I'm the one who knitted you together in your mother's womb. I'm the one who orchestrates your path. I'm the one who bought you back at a great price. I'm the one who has redeemed you. I'm the one who calls you by name. You are the apple of My eye. I'm the one who fulfills all My promises to you. I'm the one who never leaves or forsakes you. And I'm the one who loves you with an everlasting love.*

My encouragement to you is always to keep your eyes on this new family tree. With this new family tree in mind, you can know so deeply that you are the loved child of a perfect Father. You are chosen, not rejected, and you are the beneficiary of a blessing that is yours every day for the rest of your life. A blessing, as we will discover in the next chapter, that you can reach out and take hold of right now.

Chapter 7

Discovering the Perfect Father

A good friend of mine was once the athletic director at Auburn University. The first time he invited Shelley and me to a football game, we were met by his assistant, given credentials for the game—with pregame field access—and eventually escorted to his box to watch the game.

Our credentials got us onto elevators and past security checkpoints that weren't accessible to most fans attending.

While the credential had impressive powers, I noticed when I walked throughout the stadium with my friend, no one ever even bothered to check to see if I had the right badge or not. They would simply recognize the boss and smile at me because I was with him.

Over time, I've learned that it's not the badge that gives you true credibility and access in situations like these. Instead, it's your proximity to someone who is actually in charge of that world that gives you the blessing.

Why tell you this? Because it's possible that you might think the blessing we have been talking about in these pages

121

is a *thing*, like a credential you put around your neck or a VIP card you stick in your wallet. *Look everyone, I've got God's blessing. I can go anywhere in His kingdom.*

While it is true God confers benefits on us when we come to know Him (such as grace and peace and forgiveness and power), it's important to see that everything we've received is wrapped up in a *Someone*. The blessing is not a thing. The blessing is a *Person*. God is the blessing—our perfect Father.

The blessing God wants you to discover is not simply a thing He gives you—it is Himself. Yes, He will supply everything you'll ever need, yet He wants you to discover that everything you need is found *in Him*. For you to truly live out this reality you need to know who the perfect Father is. Do you know Him?

The Heart of Love

The Bible tells us that at His core, God is love. The perfect Father is loving, and when the Father acts, He always acts out of this heart of love.

That's good news for us, because at the heart of all humanity is our need for love. Maybe that's tough for you to wrap your mind around because your earthly dad couldn't get the words *I love you* out of his mouth. You wanted to hear those words so badly, and as a way of coping, you settled with the thought, *My dad isn't the kind who tells me he loves me; he just shows me.*

But we don't just want to settle for a dad who says, "You know I love you; I don't need to say it." We really need to hear it. We want to hear these words not only on monumental occasions but regularly, consistently, in both good and bad times. We want to hear those words by text and email and phone call and letter and birthday card and face-to-face around the dinner table. We don't just want empty words without actions; we want to hear him say "I love you" and show it. And wrapped throughout this desire, we want to know that something about us touches our father's heart—that there is a positive emotion inside of him when he thinks about us.

All of us processing the big ideas of this book together undoubtedly experience a whole range of thoughts and emotions about being loved. Some of us have been swimming in the ocean of a father's love for as long as we can remember. Others have literally never heard the words "I love you, son" or "I love you, baby girl" come out of our father's mouth. Some have only heard the opposite—"I hate you; I wish you'd never been born." Most of us have a mixture of good and not so good. And we all have this in common: none of our earthly fathers' love has been perfect. Yet our need to be loved—prized and valued and wanted—is at the epicenter of our hearts.

Our new story with our heavenly Father is a love-fueled story from beginning to end. It started with your conception, the moment God designed you, and the pinnacle of the story is the place where Jesus died. That moment is summed up powerfully and beautifully like this: "For God so loved the world, that He gave His only Son, so that everyone who believes in Him will not perish, but have eternal life" (John 3:16 NASB).

Packed inside this amazing love declaration is one little word, an incredibly potent little descriptor. Do you know the word?

God *sooooooooo* loved . . .

The text could just as aptly read "God loved the world." Yet this tiny little word "so" is added, a word so small it's almost completely overlooked in the text. But we can't miss it—because its ramifications for us are so huge. We need to camp out in "so land" and soak in the implications of why a great God would want to add such a tiny word to one of the most definitive proclamations of His love in the whole Bible. It's because He's trying to get through to us. He didn't merely love us. He *so* loved us. And that one little descriptor packs a terrific punch.

This love of His that compelled Him to write history around the cross of His Son was not a perfunctory love, an obligatory love that He was contractually required to offer. No, it's an emphatic love. God *sooooooooo* loved you that He gave His one and only Son. He really, really valued and prized you to the point that He gave the ultimate gift so that you could be held in His holy arms.

God's love is not vague or general. His love for you is an intense, specifically applied love.

You might be thinking, *Louie, if you knew my life, what I've been through, the things that have been done to me, you'd understand why I can't quite see how God loves me. If God loves me, then why have so many terrible things happened to me?*

One thing I hope you know by now is that this book is not my attempt to give a simplistic, surface, "churchy," or cliché answer to things you've struggled with your whole life. But I do want to offer you the reality of the cross. *Man,* you might be saying, *you've talked a lot about the cross!* Yep, I have to. Because the cross is real. The six hours in the span of history when Jesus hung on the cross say more about you than all the rest of the hours in history put together. And without a doubt, the cross says God *so* loves you.

When Shelley and I were first dating we lived a little over an hour apart. She was a student at Baylor University in Waco, Texas, and I was in grad school up the road in Fort Worth. One night while sitting in the library studying, I got the crazy idea to make a quick trip to Waco and surprise her.

I really didn't have a road trip budgeted into my schedule for the night, and I had class early the next morning. But my emotions trumped sound judgment, and within no time I was pulling up in front of her dorm. I'd stopped at the gas station nearby and picked up two cans of a soft drink we loved, and I had a plan. The mobile phone hadn't been invented, so I asked the kind woman behind the window at the desk to call Shelley's room and tell her she had a visitor and to come down to the lobby. I left the cans in plain sight (if you're wondering, it was Hawaiian Punch), and slipped out of sight around the corner. Shelley came down and saw the cans, which tipped her off that I was close by. I appeared, and we laughed and hugged (and undoubtedly kissed) as we sat side by side on the steps outside. But after about twenty minutes, our moment of togetherness was over. I had to jet because there was more studying to be done that night, and she had a test the next morning.

As I drove away, I had a final thought. The impromptu visit was a success, but how could I leave another *I love you* behind? With less than twenty bucks in my pocket, my options were limited, plus it was past eleven at night. My limited funds got me a piece of poster board from the grocery store, two markers, some nails, and a box of that stretchy plastic wrap you use when storing food in the fridge. I returned to a covered breezeway between two campus buildings and went to work.

An hour later my "I heart you" poster was finished and wrapped to protect it from the oncoming drizzle. I knew Shelley's second-floor window faced the courtyard in the middle of her quadrangle-shaped dorm. Slipping into the courtyard, I nailed my poster on the big oak tree in the center, making sure it faced her room. *Please God, don't let it get blown down during the night*, I prayed.

First thing the next morning I called her room. After a groggy hello, she finally understood what I was saying to her: "look out your window!!"

Click. I hung up and waited. I knew she only had to turn and peek through the blind.

Was the poster still there? I wondered.

A few seconds later, my phone rang.

"Awwwwww," she said. "I love you too."

I got my point across! Let it be known to all the other boys who wanted to date her—I love this girl, and she's taken! I'll hang a giant sign out in public to prove it.

I don't tell you this story to make myself look great. Shelley would add that this was well over thirty years ago, and she might ask, "What have you done lately?"

I'm telling you this story to help paint a picture of something stunning that God did for you. In fact, if you look right now, you can see the cross from wherever you are! You don't have to climb up to a holy vista or get your stuff together or be in just the perfect spot. No matter where you are—no matter how dark or lonely or awful or sinful or broken or low—if you look, you can see the cross from wherever you are. You can see God's *I love you so much* hanging on public display. His love was calculated, well-thought-out, extravagant, and costly.

You couldn't earn it. You didn't deserve it. But that didn't stop the God who *soooooooooo* loved you from giving His best so you could be born again as a daughter or son of the King!

Everybody has a Billy Graham story, and none is perhaps more poignant than the story told by his daughter Ruth at his memorial in 2018, a story that shows the essence of a father's love.

She said,

After twenty-one years my marriage ended in divorce. I was devastated. I floundered. I did a lot wrong. The rug was pulled out from under me.

My family thought it would be a good idea for me to move away, to get a fresh start somewhere else. And so, I decided to live near my older sister and her family and near a good church.

The pastor of that church introduced me to a handsome widower, and we began to date fast and furiously. My children didn't like him, but I thought, you know, they were almost grown. They didn't know—they couldn't tell me what to do. I knew what was best for my life.

My mother called me from Seattle. My father called me from Tokyo. They said, "Honey, why don't you slow down? Let us wait to get to know this man." They had never been a single parent. They had never been divorced. What did they know?

So, being stubborn, willful, and sinful I married a man—*this* man—on New Year's Eve, and within twenty-four hours I knew I'd made a terrible mistake.

After five weeks I fled. I was afraid of him. What was I going to do?

I wanted to go talk to my mother and father. It was a two-day drive. Questions swirled in my mind. What was I going to say to Daddy? What was I going to say to Mother? What was I going to say to my children?

I'd been such a failure. What were they going to say to me? "We're tired of fooling with you. We told you not to do it. You've embarrassed us."

Let me tell you. You women will understand. You don't want to embarrass your father. You really don't want to embarrass Billy Graham. And many of you know that we live on the side of a mountain, and as I wound myself up the mountain, I rounded the last bend in my father's driveway, and my father was standing there waiting for me.

As I got out of the car, he wrapped his arms around me, and he said, "Welcome home."

There was no shame. There was no blame. There was no condemnation, just unconditional love, and you know, my father was not God, but he showed me what God was like that day.

When we come to God with our sin, our brokenness, our failure, our pain and our hurt, God says, "Welcome home," and that invitation is open to you.[9]

Reason to Celebrate

The experience of Ruth Graham echoes a story Jesus told about a father with two sons. The younger son, feeling full of himself and ready to break free and see the world, asked for his share of his inheritance early. Amazingly, his dad obliged. Overnight, the boy counted the cash, quit his post on his father's estate, and headed into the distance with dreams of wild parties and total independence.

As the story goes, the money eventually ran out, the friends disappeared, and an unforeseen famine struck the land. A dejected and demoralized son hit rock bottom and turned for home.

The shocking twist in the story happens when the father doesn't condemn the son but runs down the road to meet him with open arms and the promise of a welcome-home party. The father's embrace and lavish welcome-home party stunned the community and really hacked off the older brother.

"You've never thrown me a party with my friends," he retorted when invited into the party by the father. "But this insulting, womanizing, embarrassing kid drags our family name through the mud and he gets a dance-all-night celebration."

On the surface his reaction makes total sense. But through the lens of the good news message of Jesus we see things differently. The party was a picture of the celebration of spiritual birth we have already unpacked in previous chapters. The father didn't say that the celebration was because the son "got better." He said that his son "was *dead* and is *alive* again; he was lost and is found" (Luke 15:32, emphasis mine).

Heaven celebrates when one sinner turns for home, not when religious people try harder to clean up their lives for God.

But what was up with the older brother? What was his problem? Well, it wasn't that he was slouching on the job. He worked hard every day. It wasn't that he didn't try his best. He was as straightlaced as they come. His problem, as the father tried to help him see, was that his thinking about his identity was all mixed up.

He thought he was loved *because* he showed up to work every day and was a trusted laborer. He totally missed that he was loved simply because he was a son of the father. "My son," the father said, "you are always with me, and everything I have is yours" (Luke 15:31). The older brother was working to get something he already had. He was toiling with the identity of a slave while the father saw him as a son.

So many people see God this way. They think if they try really hard, they can work their way into His good graces. But consider this: dead people can never do anything to improve their position. And without Christ, people are spiritually dead.

The beauty of this story Jesus tells us is not only that the younger son came back (though turning around and leaving behind a life of reckless choices is a necessary step in coming to God) but that the father was watching and waiting for him the whole time. The father welcomed him home because he loved him, not because he needed another hired hand on the estate.

And that's why God is pursuing you today. He doesn't want to lecture you. He wants to tell you that He loves you.

Strong Stuff

How does the perfect Father love you? Check out these Scriptures:

- God shows His love for you in that while you were still a sinner, Christ died for you. (Romans 5:8)
- Nothing can separate you from God's love. Absolutely nothing! (Romans 8:37–39)

- God's love for you is so great, it surpasses human knowledge. The love of Christ is amazingly wide and long and high and deep. (Ephesians 3:17–19)
- God loves you so much He's engraved your name on the palms of His hands. He never forgets about you. (Isaiah 49:15–16)
- He is good and kind. "The LORD your God is with you, the Mighty Warrior who saves. He will take great delight in you; in his love he will no longer rebuke you, but will rejoice over you with singing." (Zephaniah 3:17)

Can you see it? The heavenly Father is crazy about you and willing to go public with His love.

Yet all that love is for naught if we don't receive it and live in it. The echo to His great love is that we could say, "So we have come to know and to believe the love that God has for us" (1 John 4:16 ESV).

There's one more thing about our heavenly Father's love that is essential to understand and appreciate. God's love is *tough love*. He is exceedingly tender, but He's not a pushover. He's not going to just step aside and let His kids get away with whatever they decide. He loves you enough to speak sternly when appropriate, to always tell you the truth, and to discipline you when your decisions are heading you for a shipwreck. His motive will always be pure love, but God will go to great lengths to ensure your best, including saying no to something He knows is less than the best. God gave His all to love you, and more than just being loving toward you, your perfect Father is love. (Check the entire book of 1 John.)

But how do I know He won't hurt me? you ask. Because He's reaching for you with hands that have been pierced through for you. He's the one who was shattered on the cross so He could offer you a love that's indestructible, a love that will be yours from here to eternity.

God is showing you what a great place you have in His heart. Every earthly love is going to fall short at some point in time. But there's a love that is bulletproof and sure, outrageous and inviting, personal and powerful. He's the one who will never tire of saying "I love you!"

The Peak of Goodness

The perfect Father is good. This is a bottom-line truth.

One night Shelley and I were making taco salad for dinner, but there was a problem—we had no guacamole. Soon I was at our nearby grocery trying to figure out how to pick the right avocados for the job of completing our meal. I'll admit it takes a better man than me to pick an avocado that's ready to eat—not too hard, not too soft. But I was fairly confident with the four I placed in my shopping bag as I checked out and headed home.

When we cut into the first avocado, halving it to expose its big round pit, the whole thing was grayish-green and mushy inside. The pit just plopped right out on the kitchen counter. Yuck! No sweat, we had three more that looked good. We sliced into the second one, and it was worse—rotten and putrid. Somehow, in spite of all my investigative efforts, I had managed to come home with four worthless avocados. Although they looked fantastic on the outside, these avocados were no good.

A false front is definitely a bummer when the subject is fruits and vegetables, but it can be devastating when it comes to someone you trust and love.

Rest assured, God, your perfect Father, doesn't just love you with a love that looks good from a distance. Through and through, your perfect Father *is* good. You can slice and slice and slice and slice, and you're always going to find His love to be the same. Your heavenly Father is a good Father, perfect in every season.

How can we know that He is good? For one, we can come close and examine His character and actually experience His goodness. The psalmist encouraged us: "Taste and see that the LORD is good; blessed is the one who takes refuge in him" (Psalm 34:8). What an invitation! God is not afraid to invite you for a close inspection. In fact, He wants you to be close to Him. In another place the psalmist talked about how much better it is to be in God's house than anywhere else in the world. He proclaimed:

> How lovely is your dwelling place,
> LORD Almighty!
> My soul yearns, even faints,

for the courts of the LORD;

my heart and my flesh cry out

for the living God.

Even the sparrow has found a home,

and the swallow a nest for herself,

where she may have her young—

a place near your altar,

LORD Almighty, my King and my God.

(Psalm 84:1–3)

God's altar is holy, surrounded by awe and wonder. Yet even in that holy place you will find a welcome mat for all looking for a home—for all seeking to be close to their Maker. Even the swallow can build her nest there, "near your altar, LORD Almighty." If a tiny bird can come near to Him, you know that's where God wants His sons and daughters to be. He wants them right by His side.

God invites us to *taste and see*. God wants His love to be experienced. He wants you to bite off a chunk of His character through the pages of His Word and the person of Christ. He wants you to chew on His attributes—to dwell on who He is. He doesn't want to be reduced to information you read on a page. God wants you to look up from the pages of Scripture with the eyes of your heart and realize He is right there with you.

To say that God is good speaks to His motives, to His intent, although not everything in life is good. In fact, the world is badly broken. But in a world filled with wrong, your Father is still good. As we come closer to Him and realize that what is on the inside matches the promise we heard from a distance, we come to the same conclusion as the psalmist:

> Better is one day in your courts
> than a thousand elsewhere;
> I would rather be a doorkeeper in the house of
>   my God
> than dwell in the tents of the wicked.
> For the LORD God is a sun and shield;
> the LORD bestows favor and honor;
> no good thing does he withhold
> from those whose walk is blameless.
> LORD Almighty,
> blessed is the one who trusts in you.
>
>   (Psalm 84:10–12)

Another way we know God is good is by taking a quick survey of His résumé. It's not like He's been around only a decade or two. Our sample of His life and motives is not small. God has been around since before time.

Maybe in the short term, like this week or this year, we're not positive that everything happening around us anthems the fact that God is good. Sometimes we just can't see it. We don't understand. Yet we have a rich history of God's activity preserved in the pages of Scripture, and we can look back over the ages and see the goodness of His love.

Staying Power

Think for a moment how everything beautiful in life has an expiration date—a moment when even fine things wilt and decay and die. It's true of the flowers blooming in your garden, the meal you're cooking for dinner, your loved ones, and even you. Scripture even tells us that one day the whole earth is going to fade away.

But we don't have to worry or fear, because every step of the way our perfect Father will be good. And when the end comes, He will take us to a new forever with Him (a brand-new heaven and earth) where every bad thing that sin has brought into our lives will be vanquished. Until then you can be sure that everything that happens to you will pass through His goodness and His love. Nothing will stop your Father from bringing about good in your life, no matter what.

He says, "'For I know the plans I have for you,' declares the LORD, 'plans to prosper you and not to harm you, plans to give you hope and a future'" (Jeremiah 29:11).

And He promises "that in all things God works for the good of those who love him, who have been called according to his purpose" (Romans 8:28).

Again, we anchor our hope in the cross, the place where our perfect Father places every anti-good thing on His innocent Son so that you can know His love, experience His forgiveness, and know that He is good.

So maybe your dad was/is a good guy! If that's the case, I'm so happy for you. But maybe your earthly dad was a bad man.

Not good, through and through. If so, I don't want to just blow by this moment and offer a bunch of nice-sounding words that you feel like are a million miles away from your reality. Though it may sound a little crazy, I want you to try something.

Just pause for a moment and let your mind drift back over two thousand years to a hill outside Jerusalem. I want you to dwell on the very moment God revealed His master plan to the world. It wasn't a power play like we might expect, where God would swoop in and wipe everyone out. He was coming to serve us, not to squash us. So our perfect Father offered the only good person alive to die in our place. He didn't do it against the will of His Son. Jesus signed off on the mission, a mission of love and justice, stamping out the lingering effects of sin that had cursed us to die.

As you think about what happened there, listen to the pounding of the nails as they smash through Jesus' hands and feet and into the beams of wood. *Clink. Clink. Clink. Clink.* Every blow is telling you right now that God is Someone you can trust, Someone who is never going to let you down. And when He reaches out His hand to you and says, "Come close, walk with Me," you can know His hand is one you can hold on to forever.

The perfect Father's arms are strong, and His heart is good.

Everything in His Hands

The perfect Father is sovereign. That means simply that God is great—really great. In fact, His sovereignty means He is the

The perfect Father's
arms are strong

and
His
heart
is
good.

greatest force in the universe. He sees everything. He understands it all. He stitches together generations and millennia and galaxies and time into a story of His love and grace.

How great is He? God invented the inventors. He created the laboratory of the cosmos and the science used by the scientists. He scans all of human history as easily as we would a ten-second commercial ad before a news clip. He holds the universe between His fingers. He calls the shots, and at this very moment He is standing at the end of human history, waiting for us to arrive at His predetermined conclusion. To say it another way—if you know Him, it's your Father who runs the world. And He is the loving, good one.

As we've just highlighted, the fact that a great and good God is holding the world in His hands does not mean that everything in the universe is good. No, sin hit the world like a wrecking ball in an attempt to shatter God's best-laid intentions for you and me. Yet even this was no surprise to God, and no evil can force His hand or stymie His plans. God had rescue in mind before the fall of mankind. Scripture says that Christ was "slain from the creation of the world" (Revelation 13:8). God is good, and He trumps the power of the darkness. He is good, and He brings beauty from the ashes. God is in control and, as Job discovered, "No purpose of [His] can be thwarted" (Job 42:2).

So how does your Father's sovereignty impact you as a son or daughter? How does it change the way you live to know you are a child of the sovereign King? For one thing, you can have confidence that God always has a plan, and His plan will always come to pass. That doesn't mean God is going to explain everything to us on this side of heaven. It just assures us in every situation that this loving, good, great, perfect Father is painting something beautiful on a canvas bigger than we can see or understand.

One night my mom and I sat in a tiny consultation room at the hospital at about 9:00 p.m. My dad had been suffering the effects of a previously undetected brain infection for days, maybe longer. As he lay in a coma in an ICU room down the hallway, we were face-to-face with a neurosurgeon we'd never met before. He told us my dad's brain was swelling and he needed us to sign a piece of paper giving him permission to remove a portion of my dad's brain. If he didn't perform this operation, he announced, my dad most likely wouldn't make it through the night.

I signed the paper.

It's a miracle my dad survived the surgery and the viral attack that normally would take the life of someone his age. Yet the effects of the procedure and the damage already done by the virus-induced swelling (not to mention the stroke my dad suffered the day following the surgery) left him physically and mentally disabled. My genius, designer, golfing dad never returned to work, drove a car, or dressed unassisted again.

Our family was in shock for a long time, wondering when we'd wake up to our old lives again. But each new day only brought trials, frustration, more hospital stays, another brain operation, rehab centers, questions.

When Dad first became disabled, Shelley and I were

living in Texas, leading a ministry for college students on the campus where I hung that "I heart you" poster on the oak tree. Now, as the years of hardship rolled by, Shelley and I continually asked God to release us from our ministry at Baylor so we could move to Atlanta and help Mom take care of Dad. But every time we asked, the answer was a clear *not now*.

Finally, in November of the seventh year of my dad's disability, we got what we thought was the go-ahead to move to Atlanta. We were thrilled. We'd be sad to leave behind the work we'd built for ten years, but the calling to help with my dad was strong. We planned to finish out the spring semester and then head to Atlanta to give Mom a much-needed hand.

Our last meeting of the spring was on Monday, May 1, and it was going to be a huge thank-you celebration for all God had done in the decade we'd been serving there. Lots of friends planned to be there, and our ministry board would attend. We planned a really special night.

We've heard that last gathering was incredible. But oddly, Shelley and I were not there.

You're thinking, *You missed your own goodbye party?*

Yep.

That Monday was the day we buried my father. He had a heart attack and died the previous Friday before we could make it home to help with his care. Talk about being frustrated and confused. My dad was gone, and that was more pain than I knew existed. Added to that, we had already said goodbye to a ministry we really loved, and there was no turning back now.

So we moved to Atlanta even though Dad was gone. Turned out, Mom needed a lot of help reentering a world she'd basically pulled out of altogether to give Dad the twenty-four seven care he required. But I was frustrated. Did I miss out on God's timing completely? Were we supposed to go to Atlanta straightaway in November? If we had done that, we'd have been there the last few months with Dad. How could I have messed this up?

I wasn't so much mad at God as I was disappointed in myself. But we trudged on to our new city, wondering what we were supposed to do next. It's a long (and incredible) story that I can't spell out completely here without writing another book, but a few months after my father died, God dropped a vision onto our radar that in time became Passion Conferences and everything else associated with Passion. Since that time God has gathered millions of university-aged young people at Passion events around the world, calling them to live for what matters most.

Yet in the summer after my father left us, the idea of Passion was only that—an idea—and we had no way of knowing what to do next. But chasing and building the Passion vision turned out to be a new venture, a new beginning.

Fast-forward to the year 2013, eighteen years later. We were walking into what would be our largest gathering of college students to date as upward of sixty thousand university students were set to unite in the former Georgia Dome in Atlanta.

The night before, a college football bowl game was played

on the very field where we would gather the next day. The game ended late, and we didn't get the venue to begin our setup until around midnight. Interestingly, I'd been asked to give the invocation before that game (one of the few sporting events of this magnitude that still opens with a prayer), and I had stood out near midfield, close to the fifty-yard line.

The next time I walked onto that field it had been transformed. Overnight a thick plastic cover had been placed on the turf in pieces that resembled a jigsaw puzzle. Then a huge circular stage was set up in the middle of the field, with accompanying lights and sound and everything needed to translate the music and message of the conference to the tens of thousands of people that would fill the stadium.

That night as I walked to the steps leading up to the stage during the opening session, my heart almost stopped beating. It was the biggest event we had ever hosted. The moment was filled with possibility and expectation. I was about to deliver a message that I was praying would forever change the direction of the people who were gathered there. But I had to stop and catch my breath for another reason.

In the frenzy following the end of the game the night before, there had been no time to erase the logo of the bowl game's sponsor from the center of the field. It was still there, underneath the plastic covering and *directly* underneath the stage where I was about to stand.

WHAT!?!?!

In that instant I realized the Chick-fil-A logo (they were the sponsors of the game), which my dad had created in 1964, was now painted on the field directly under the stage at the largest Passion Conference to date. For four days I would stand and preach and lead on top of my dad's design, his creation.

I could hardly believe what was happening. What are the odds of something like that happening?

And then I remembered that my perfect Father is a sovereign King. This crazy collision of my dad's logo design and the fulfillment of the vision that sprang from the bitter soil that accompanied his death didn't resolve the suffering that our family, and especially my dad, had endured. It wasn't like I got an explanation from heaven for why everything happened the way it did. But it was a reminder to me of God being loving and good. It was my perfect Father reminding me that all the frayed stories called "life on earth" are not so disconnected in His sovereign plans.

God knows the "end from the beginning" (Isaiah 46:10). With Him "one day is like a thousand years, and a thousand years like one day" (2 Peter 3:8 NASB). "He determines the number of the stars and calls them each by name" (Psalm 147:4), so there's no way He will ever forget your name. And He's always working for your good and His glory. Your perfect Father is actually working all around you right now. And nothing is going to stop Him from making you the son or daughter He's dreamed you can be.

You may not get a clear blueprint for your life today. Instead, you may just get curveballs and left turns you didn't see coming. But can you see that your Father is above it all, in it all, working through it all? To know Him more and more as the sovereign King will bring peace and confidence in every storm and every season. To believe that He is loving, good, and in control will allow you to do well with what He has placed in your hands today, leaving all the outcomes to Him.

But there's even more to discover about the perfect Father.

Chapter 8

Appreciating the Flawless Father

In his book *The God You Can Know*, my mentor Dan DeHaan shares an illustration that seems appropriate here. He talks about a boy who is fishing in a small pond, moving around the shore from spot to spot until he's exhausted every inch only to discover a small stream flowing from the pond. As he follows the stream, it widens into a creek and then a river, eventually leading him to the sea. The body of water he thought he knew in full was only the beginning of a much greater world to be discovered.

The same could be said of my efforts to describe the perfect Father. Trying to exhaust God's character in a few chapters of this book is like me trying to fit the ocean into a fishbowl on your coffee table. But let's dive a little deeper into God's heart and character. Let's discover more of who God is so you can know who is inviting you into this new relationship as a son or daughter of a perfect Father.

The Perfect Father Is a Provider

One of Jesus' most well-known teachings—the Sermon on the Mount—gives an amazing look at how God the perfect Father operates. Jesus was describing God to His disciples, encouraging them to trust God in prayer, to go to God and find out that God does not disappoint.

Jesus said,

> Ask and it will be given to you; seek and you will find; knock and the door will be opened to you. For everyone who asks receives; the one who seeks finds; and to the one who knocks, the door will be opened. (Matthew 7:7–8)

Immediately after Jesus laid this foundation, He turned the subject specifically toward fatherhood. Jesus asked the crowd, "Which of you, if your son asks for bread, will give him a stone? Or if he asks for a fish, will give him a snake?" (Matthew 7:9–10).

Those are rhetorical questions, with obvious answers. It's almost as if Jesus was telling a joke. He was saying, "Look, if your child comes to you at mealtime and says, 'Daddy, I'm hungry. Can I have some bread, please?' no parent is going to hand the child a rock and say, 'I hope you like your dinner crunchy. Eat up, son.' Or if your child's stomach is rumbling and she asks for a piece of broiled fish, you're not going to hand her a rattlesnake and say, 'Watch out—live snake! And he bites!'"

I imagine the crowd chuckled at Jesus' comparisons. They understood the lesson. Jesus spelled it out further, saying, "If you, despite being evil, know how to give good gifts to your children, how much more will your Father who is in heaven give good things to those who ask Him!" (Matthew 7:11 NASB).

The lesson is clear. If human parents, with a propensity toward sin, know what good things to give a child when the child asks, how much more will God the perfect Father "[provide] us with everything for our enjoyment" (1 Timothy 6:17)? God is the giver of good gifts.

That's not to say that God will hand us a Ferrari if we pray for one. But it does mean that God always provides what is best for us—and more than a bare subsistence, He provides us things for our enjoyment. He even provides you with "the desires of your heart" (Psalm 37:4).

Some of you might be thinking, *I hate to break it to you, Louie. But my dad actually did give me a rock when I needed bread. My dad handed out snakes right and left. If I asked for simple things I needed, he gave me things so twisted they were unthinkable.*

Others of you who've experienced the benefit of a generous earthly father face a different challenge. You found your security in what your earthly dad could give you and never learned to be dependent on God. Yet many of you are coming from a place where your dad never provided even the essentials.

If that's the case, it might actually be hard for you to feel confident about having the basics in life. But the perfect Father doesn't want you living with a scarcity mentality, constantly worrying about whether you'll have what you need. The key to transforming our thoughts about "father" is found in the phrase that Jesus used in the passage about the snakes and rocks. Look closely at three important words: *how much more*. Notice, "How much more will your Father who is in heaven give good things to those who ask him!" (Matthew 7:11).

That's Jesus saying, Look, in the normal course of life, earthly fathers typically know how to meet their children's needs. And on most occasions, parents will do this, even though the good ones sometimes mess up, and the bad ones blast the picture all to smithereens. Yet your heavenly Father will meet needs, and "how much more!" The invitation is to see the heavenly Father as the perfect provider. Remember, He's not the *reflection* of your earthly dad. He's the *perfection* of fatherhood.

When we start soaking in the truth that God is a flawless Father, not a busted-up earthly father, then without a doubt we can trust our heavenly Father. He doesn't sin. He doesn't make mistakes. God our heavenly Father cares for us perfectly. He calls us "children of God" and "lavishes" His love upon us, and "how much more" will He provide for us. His motives are always pure, His actions are always flawless, and His intentions are always good toward us.

A Flawless Record

Looking at what He has done in the past helps us know that we can depend on Him in the future. He once fed thousands with a snack from a kid in the crowd. He took the five small loaves of bread and two tiny fish in His hands, offered thanks, and proceeded to break them again and again until everyone had more than enough. For good measure there were twelve baskets left over. Did Jesus miscount? Nope. He did this to show you that your Father is a God of abundance, not scarcity. And that He wants you to take on a generosity mentality that helps you see beyond your own needs to the needs of others.

Another time Jesus was at a wedding when the wine ran out and the host started to panic. Jesus told the servants to fill large pots with water, then He turned the water into wine. And not just any kind of wine! The guests were amazed that their host had saved the best for last. When the party is winding down, who comes through with the best you can offer? The Father who provides.

Every day of my life growing up we had a roof over our heads, and though we were definitely lower-middle class, we had everything we needed. Both Mom and Dad worked most all those years to make sure we didn't go without. But there wasn't anything extravagant in the equation, and it wasn't until I was in college that we moved into a real house (a townhouse), with a second floor and a legitimate front door and foyer. We pretty much lived paycheck to paycheck without a lot of margin, and it wasn't unlike Dad to take out a loan from the credit union at his work to cover the big-ticket items like a "new" used car or a wedding.

That may be our situation in our human family, but when

it comes to your new family tree, a son or daughter of the King never has to just scrape by. Your soul is provided for lavishly, and God feeds and clothes your spirit with abundance. After all, you're a child of the King. Wait a minute—wonderful for our *souls*, but what about our *bodies*? They, too, have needs, and there are certainly times when Christians live in less than abundant circumstances, even in poverty or starvation. Does God care about those human needs?

Let's be clear: God doesn't live paycheck to paycheck, because He doesn't get paid. Who would pay Him anyway? He already owns everything there is to own. And He's committed to His children. So you don't have to hoard your goods, and you don't have to worry about tomorrow. Notice what Jesus said:

> Therefore I tell you, do not worry about your life, what you will eat or drink; or about your body, what you will wear. Is not life more than food, and the body more than clothes? Look at the birds of the air; they do not sow or reap or store away in barns, and yet your heavenly Father feeds them. Are you not much more valuable than they? Can any one of you by worrying add a single hour to your life? (Matthew 6:25–27)

This is clearly about human, material needs. And notice how Jesus turned this promise toward you with this question—"Are you not much more valuable than they?" Again, He's not waiting for an answer. Jesus is making a declaration. The perfect Father may not give you everything you want, right when you want it. But He's not going to leave you hanging. There will never be a gravestone to mark His death (they tried that at the garden tomb, but death couldn't keep Jesus in the grave!). He's never going to be too busy at work to care about you, or too weak or unmotivated or too broken-down to notice you and step in to provide all you need. Even the very human troubles of poverty, cancer, divorce, and the like can never touch us without being first filtered through His love, for His good purposes. The perfect Father is loving and good and in control.

And He is going to make certain you have everything you need, even if your need is to experience a time of want so that you can draw closer to Him.

The Perfect Father Is Able

Many of us who grew up learning about Jesus have heard about a guy named Zacchaeus. Some of you instantly might be singing in your head, *Zacchaeus was a wee little man.* The story goes like this: As Jesus was passing through a certain town, a great crowd lined the streets to get a look at Him. Jesus had been doing miracles from place to place, and His reputation preceded Him. The problem was that Zacchaeus was a short little dude and couldn't see over the crowd. Not to worry; he shimmied up a nearby tree and actually had the best view of all as Jesus passed by. Shockingly, Jesus stopped right in front of that tree and called Zacchaeus by name. Then Jesus did something unusual—He invited Himself to stay at Zacchaeus's house.

"Hey Zacchaeus, how's it going?" Jesus called. "Come down quick. I'm staying at your place tonight!" The crowd froze in disbelief.

They didn't freeze because Jesus was being a little forward by inviting Himself to this man's house but because they knew Zacchaeus was the chief taxman in town. Not only did he work for the authorities; he was getting filthy rich by taking a cut of the tax he was charging. All those standing along the road stared in stunned silence. *Ummm. I think You picked the wrong guy, Jesus,* they murmured under their breath. *This guy's a cheat, the worst sinner in town!*

He Knows Your Name

What does this story have to say about God being able? One simple thing it shows us is that God knew Zacchaeus by name. God's memory never fails, and He's never had to lean over to an angel to ask, *Who's that tall girl over there with the sunglasses?* The perfect Father has instant awareness of all information at all times.

Recently, researchers at York University found that our brains can remember ten thousand faces over the course of a lifetime. The average person, the study discovered, can recall around five thousand, but scientists say that doesn't mean we'll always remember their names.[10] Man, that's a relief. I'm pretty sure I can't remember five thousand people by name! But the perfect Father can. He knows the name of every person He's created and their exact location on planet Earth every instant.

It's possible your earthly father has seemed to forget about you. But not the perfect, faultless Father. Jesus didn't need advanced prep from His team on the name of the little tax guy. He could have named every person in town. And He didn't need directions to Zacchaeus's house or anyone else's.

On another occasion Jesus sat down by a well to rest while His disciples went into the town ahead to get something to eat. Soon He was in conversation with a lady that led to an extraordinary offer. He promised her the hope of living water that would satisfy the deep thirst in her soul. The woman said, "Sir, give me this water so that I won't get thirsty and have to keep coming here to draw water" (John 4:15), not fully understanding what Jesus was trying to say. He told her to go get her husband and then He'd give her the "living water."

"I don't have a husband," she told Him.

Jesus didn't fall for it. Why? Because He's able, which means that He knows everything about us. He knew this woman's name just like He knew Zacchaeus's name. And He also knew that when it came to marriage, she'd struck out five times and she and the guy she was living with weren't married.

Uh-oh. *This guy has been reading my mail*, she thought. She decided He must be a prophet, but Jesus was even more. He was God in human flesh, a reflection of the perfect Father. He knows who you are and understands everything about what you do.

Jesus Can Relate

But we see something else about the perfect Father in this woman's story as well as in the story of Zacchaeus: God is comfortable in the real world. He's not afraid to mix it up with anyone and everyone. Jesus invited Himself to the house of a tax accountant, a numbers guy.

Really? What would they possibly talk about? How could Jesus hold His own? Wouldn't Jesus be better off sticking with Bible trivia? What would Jesus know about income tax credits, the accrual basis of accounting, limited liability companies, or short-term capital gains? Shouldn't He stay in the spiritual zone?

Nope. He's well-read, super current, and fully up to speed on your situation.

And what's with this ability of His to know all about messy marriage situations?

An incredible thing about this perfect Father God—and an underappreciated benefit for many people who claim to follow Him—is that He knows everything about everything. He's just as comfortable talking to you about British baking, building a rocket, breaking par on the golf course, binary math, baby strollers, bipartisan legislation, or bipolar symptoms as He is reciting the books of the Bible. He's down with graphic art, micro-business, crop management, knitting (even the loop stitch), supply-side economics, bioethics, urban design, bird migration, shiplap renovation, or whatever currently occupies your thinking.

You don't need to inform God of anything or teach Him

how to operate the remote or post on social media. He is well able on His own. But more, He's interested in you and whatever you are passionate about. That's not to say He's eager to condone whatever you're producing or the way you're going about your work. But if you have a passion for architecture or artificial intelligence or raising a family, a passion that He has woven into your heart to bring light to the world, He's the Father you've been looking for.

A Helping Hand

There's one last thing about His ability I want us to see: the reality that the perfect Father is able tells us He has the power to assist us in any area of our lives. Both Zacchaeus's story and that of the woman at the well ended in miracles of personal transformation.

You'd think that if the Son of God went to dinner at a tax collector's house it would end in disaster. And if Jesus met a five-time divorcée on the street, you'd expect an extravaganza of shame and condemnation. But both people found healing and freedom through their encounters with Jesus. Sure, Jesus could talk about tax issues all night long, and He could recount the details of every shattered marriage the woman had endured. Yet He didn't just come to prove that He was aware of their circumstances, He came to change their lives for the better. And He had the power and authority to do so.

I was at a music event recently where a little eight-year-old girl couldn't see the stage, so she asked her dad to pick her up so she could see. In one motion he hoisted her high in the air and sat her up on his shoulders. By now she was about eight feet tall, a few feet higher than everyone else in the crowd. The dad's smile told me he was so glad his daughter had a better view, but he was equally proud she had asked for him to flex his might and do something she couldn't do.

A good dad doesn't despise his little kid's request for help. He loves it. In the same way, God is not annoyed by your requests. He's happy you came to Him and thrilled that you thought of Him as able and willing to help.

The flawless Father is able to do what no one else can do for you. Beyond the cross of Christ, there's an equally significant moment in time that lets you know that God is able—it's the moment God raised Jesus from the grave.

Through the Power of an Empty Tomb

That heavy stone the guards used to seal the tomb where Jesus' dead body lay was easily moved by an angel sent by the perfect Father. The demonstration of God's ability wasn't moving the stone. God had already done the more miraculous work when He called forth His Son from the depths of hades. The powers of darkness trembled as sin and hell were defeated; Jesus was alive forever, a victorious champion over sin and death.

When our eyes are open with the new "revelation sight" we talked about earlier, we come to see this: God's power is limitless and His arm is mighty to save. We've already highlighted this passage where Paul encouraged us to see with new eyes, but it's worth repeating:

> I pray that the eyes of your heart may be enlightened in order that you may know the hope to which he has called you, the riches of his glorious inheritance in his holy people, and his incomparably great power for us who believe. That power is the same as the mighty strength he exerted when he raised Christ from the dead and seated him at his right hand in the heavenly realms, far above all rule and authority, power and dominion, and every name that is invoked, not only in the present age but also in the one to come. (Ephesians 1:18–21)

God wants us to see how great His power (ability) is and to know we have access to that power in Christ.

Paul also said, "And if the Spirit of him who raised Jesus from the dead is living in you, he who raised Christ from the dead will also give life to your mortal bodies because of his Spirit who lives in you" (Romans 8:11).

Mark gave an account in chapter nine of his gospel about a man whose son was possessed by an evil spirit. Jesus' disciples prayed for the son but to no avail. When Jesus arrived, everyone was arguing about why the boy wasn't getting free. Jesus asked the boy's father, "How long has he been like this?"

"From childhood," he answered. "It has often thrown him into fire or water to kill him. But if you can do anything, take pity on us and help us."

Notice the father said to Jesus *if you can*, meaning, *if you are able.*

"If you can?" said Jesus. "Everything is possible for one who believes."

The father was honest and said, "I do believe; help my unbelief."

That's probably where we all are to one degree or another—somewhere between belief and unbelief. I pray that as you take this journey, your eyes will open to see that the perfect Father, who is loving and good, the One who is in control, will provide everything you need. That Father is able to do all He says He can do.

The Perfect Father Is Present

We all long for our earthly fathers to participate actively in our world. Above all, we don't want to be left alone. We want our earthly dad to put down his phone, stop scrolling the news on his tablet, mute the TV, and truly listen to us. We want him to show up at our basketball games. We want him to remember to call on our birthdays. We want him to visit the hospital when our first baby is born. We want our dad to be there in the important moments. It's part of his blessing. His active participation demonstrates to us that we are important in his world. We matter.

Every earthly dad can't be present all the time. Like mine can't. He's never showing up for an important event in my life again. He's gone. But there are other reasons dads don't show up. Some are outside of our fathers' control. Business meetings are a part of the fabric of life, and airline flights get canceled. Even the divorce that's wrecked your family tree might not be your dad's desire. Maybe your mom's the one who lost the plot, or cheated on the family, or fell into a pattern of abuse or addiction. It's possible your dad is eager to lavish you with his love (and does his best from afar), but a custody settlement prevents him from being a part of your day-to-day life.

Other dads have chosen to opt out. Distance grows over time and, as a result, Dad doesn't always show up when you need him to. Worse, some dads check out of our lives altogether.

But the perfect Father remains present with us. In fact, this has been a trait of our God from the beginning. In the garden, God walked with the first humans in the cool of the day. When His people were navigating the desert after being freed from bondage, God had Moses build a Tent of Meeting where His presence descended in a cloud that covered the tent as God talked with Moses face-to-face. In time, the tent was replaced by a tabernacle, and then a temple, and in each place, there was the promise of God's presence.

One night in Bethlehem things changed—Christ was born. God was no longer in a tent or a temple, not in the cloud or some other manifestation of His nearness. God was now among men in the person of Jesus, whose name is called Emmanuel—God with us.

The psalmist encouraged us, speaking about the perfect

Father, "In your presence there is fullness of joy; at your right hand are pleasures forevermore" (Psalm 16:11 ESV). Now, in Christ we have the promise, "I will never leave you nor forsake you" (Hebrews 13:5 ESV). Nowhere in the New Testament do we have the imagery of God's presence like we find in the Old Testament, or even a single invitation to seek His presence. Why is this? Does God's presence not matter anymore?

Of course it does, but because God is now among men, we see that through the Spirit of God and the person of Christ, He is living in the hearts of believers. This is how we know we will never be alone—because Christ lives in us.

We can still feel lonely, especially when we drift away from true community with God's people, losing touch with the Spirit and the Word. But God never leaves. He is always there. Yes, there are times when we sense that God is near more than others, like that sense of knowing that someone you love just walked into the room. But the joy of that moment is discovering the person you sensed walking into the room is *actually* in the room with you. "I sensed your presence," you might say, "but I'm so glad you are here."

Although Jesus is not physically with you, He has given you "another Helper" who is with you forever—God the Holy Spirit. God is actually everywhere all the time. And we believe that He is with us in a powerful way as His Spirit takes up residence in our lives. A shift happens, and we understand that life is not so much "Jesus *and* me" as

Matthew 7:11

...how much
more
will your
Father
who is in
heaven
give what is
good
to those who
ask Him!

it is "Jesus *in* me." As the Spirit fills us, we grow to know what it means to sense that He is near in sunny days and stormy nights. The perfect Father is closer than a phone call away.

He is in you and with you at all times. This is why we keep circling the plane around this central truth:

> Though my father and mother forsake me, the LORD will receive me. (Psalm 27:10)

Those words aren't a prescription for a magical happy pill—if one even existed. Those words are about us developing real faith, a raw faith, a faith where we acknowledge the Lord even though the people who are supposed to be the closest to us have instead turned their backs on us. In the case of this psalm, an earthly father and mother have forsaken their own child.

We don't know the specific reason for the forsaking described in this psalm, but maybe the father wasn't there when he was needed, or perhaps the father was abusive, or the father was passive, and perhaps the mother stepped in and tried to help. That's what often happens today. Mothers can be awesome, and mothers can see when a father isn't what he needs to be. Plenty of mothers try to stand in that gap, and some succeed in big ways, others in partial ways. But maybe this mother finally gave up and said, *Nope, can't do it anymore.* Or maybe she never even tried to step in and was actually hurtful toward her child from the start. Maybe the mother was gone, or the mother was off-kilter, or the mother was abusive along with the father. Any way you look at it, there's a huge amount of pain wrapped up in the words of that psalm. Yet the Lord hasn't abandoned this person. The Lord "receives" this person. The ESV translates that word this way: "The LORD will take me in." The NLT reads: "The LORD will hold me close."

That's good news, but sadly, the initial pain expressed in that verse reflects the reality of this planet, because sure enough, bad things happen on a broken planet. God, in His infinite wisdom, has given people freedom of choice. Some people choose to bless others with their freedom of choice. Others choose to hurt people. There's a lot of injustice in this world. A lot of poor choices and heartache. Fortunately, the Bible says that one day, all things will be made new (Revelation 21:1–8). One day, everything will be made right (Isaiah 61). One day, justice will "roll on like a river, and righteousness like a never-failing stream!" (Amos 5:24).

Even today, despite all the pain in the world, God is greater than all our pain. He's greater than our greatest wounds and hurts. God is always nearby so we can turn to Him, and when we turn, God receives us. He takes us in and holds us close. God draws us into His arms, a loved child of the Creator of the universe. The perfect Father is loving and good. He is in control and will provide everything we need. The perfect Father is able, and He is always with us.

The Perfect Father Is a Protector

Everyone who has lost a dad, either to divorce, disinterest, death, or distance, has a special place in God's heart. He is committed to you. The psalmist described this care powerfully:

> Sing to God, sing in praise of his name,
> extol him who rides on the clouds;
> rejoice before him—his name is the LORD.
> A father to the fatherless, a defender of widows,
> is God in his holy dwelling.
> God sets the lonely in families,
> he leads out the prisoners with singing. (Psalm 68:4–6)

For openers, our invitation is to begin with praise because He alone is worthy of our worship. Specifically, we are invited to extol the one who "rides on the clouds." That's some incredible songwriting imagery. We are called to sing to this God and sing praises to His name. But it can be hard to join God's song when we're hurting inside.

God is singing over us, and sometimes all we can do is receive His words of love, and that is enough. We have turned toward God in our pain and He's caught us up and is holding us close, and then a long, long time needs to go by before we can do anything other than listen to His voice.

Yet somewhere within our healing, we sense the invitation to sing praise to God, the perfect Father who's already singing over us. When we begin to praise and worship Him, our healing is somehow accelerated. Our eyes are lifted off of ourselves. We're invited to look at the perfect, flawless Father, who isn't afraid of a dark night.

I have a good friend who is a father of little children, and he tells me that sometimes on stormy nights, when his children can't sleep, he goes into his kids' bedroom and sings to them, then invites his children to sing along with him. He explains how something reassuring happens in those moments. He sings worship songs to God, songs the kids have heard at church. The children hear the voice of their father, strong and reassuring, and the children hear their own voices, too, joining in along with the sound of strength and reassurance. When the children start singing, additional comfort transfers to the children. The children aren't afraid of the storm as much. The children hear words of praise come from their own mouths. The children are reminded that their father is close to them and that this storm, too, will pass.

The next part of Psalm 68 holds forth the truth that God is especially in tune with the fatherless. He's especially close to those who are widows, to those who don't have families they can rely on. He's especially compassionate to those who are held captive—either by their own sins or perhaps by the sins of others. God the perfect Father is the defender of people who need defending. He's the one who abolishes loneliness, the one who breaks the chains of bondage. This is the same God who rides on the clouds, the same God who invites us close to Him, the same God who sings over us and calls us His sons and daughters.

In the culture in which Psalm 68 was first written, the worst-case scenario for anybody was to be fatherless or a widow. You were basically left to fend for yourself. You were pushed out of society, and you didn't have a chance to get ahead. In many situations, the same is true today. And in these especially needy scenarios, God reaches down to people who are feeling low and living low. He sets the lowly within families. He rejoices over us with song. He starts the song because of His love for us, and then He invites us to sing along with Him.

That all sounds good, Louie, but where was God when I needed defending? Where was He when I cried out for help and nothing happened?

If that's what you're asking right now, I would agree those are big and painful questions. Again, I won't try to gloss over what has happened to you. But the fact that you are reading these words means this: you made it through the pain. You're here now. And though there are painful memories and scars, God has brought you through to a new day.

Remember those times you told yourself, *I won't make it another day?* But you did, and you are still standing. I believe you are still reading, still searching, still hoping (if you're not hoping for a healing, you wouldn't have made it this far in this book), and still reaching because God was there even though it didn't look like He was. He was giving you the strength to endure and probably even protecting you from greater harm in ways you didn't know.

Then why didn't He stop what was happening to me? Isn't that the biggest question of all?

I think the answer is because the moment He steps in and removes all the collateral damage of this broken world from ever happening again, that will mark the instant life on earth is over. And in that moment the lost will be lost forever and many whom God wanted to become sons and daughters will be separated from His arms. So He waits and extends grace another day. And for twenty-four more hours we are caught in the crossfire of a sin-shattered world.

But today He is reaching with strong arms to pick up any who are fatherless, and He's standing with resolve to defend every widow. It doesn't have to be death that creates widows and orphans. In reality, every divorce, in some way, leaves widows and orphans in its wake. Yet God rides in on the clouds announcing that He wants to be a father to the fatherless.

Is it you He's coming for right now? Are you feeling lonely and without a family? If so, His eyes are on you and His arms are outstretched. He's the perfect Father, the one who is loving and good and in control. The one who will provide everything you need. He's the Father who is able and who is with you and who has been fighting for you every moment of your life.

Just think: God has an individual plan for your life. He knew you even before you were born, and all the days you'll live were chronicled in His book before one of them came to be (Psalm 139:16).

God began a good work in you, and He'll finish what He started (Philippians 1:6).

God has prepared an incredible future for you. It's so amazing that no mind has ever conceived it (1 Corinthians 2:7–9).

God has chosen you to live a fruitful, effective, God-honoring life (John 15:16).

That's why He'll never back down from any threat to you, His child. He's already overcome the greatest dangers you'll ever face—sin and death. And He won't stop now. He is the perfect Father. He will protect you as you go because He has a purpose and plan for your life.

At the center of God's plan is the hope that you will grow up to look like and act like Him.

Chapter 9

Growing Up
Like Dad

Like you, I have a physical birth certificate—an actual paper
copy. I haven't seen it in a while, but when I was growing
up you needed that piece of paper for all kinds of things—to
prove your age at Little League tryouts, to register the first day
of class at school, to get your driver's license.

Your birth certificate, like mine, primarily declares that you
were in fact *born*! You didn't just mysteriously arrive on planet
Earth; rather, at such and such hospital, and at such and such
time, you joined the human race. A quick glance at the birth
certificate will tell us your length at birth and how much you
weighed. A footprint may be there to forever link you to the
information. And then, the two most powerful things about you
are listed: the names of your mom and dad. In some cases the
dad's name may not be recorded if the parents are not married,
but this document tells you by whom you came to be and says a
lot about what you're going to be like. In physical terms you don't
have much of a choice, given that you are the result of the com-
bining of your parents' DNA, the combination of their genes.

Family Resemblance

When you put it in the most basic biological terms, it goes like this: you received something from your mom and something from your dad, and the result of the two is 100 percent you. That's why, like it or not, you have a strong tendency to grow up to look like, be like, and act like your mom and dad.

Say this to a teenager and they are likely to fight you over it, defying the power of genetics and swearing they are *definitely not* ever going to look like their mom or dad. But let a few years go by between visits at Thanksgiving, and Aunt Lucinda will make things clear enough as she comes through the door, gets one look at the fourteen-year-old you, and declares excitedly—*I can hardly believe it! You look just like your mother!*

This kind of proclamation isn't necessarily what every teen is hoping to have said about them (they might be thinking they're a lot more cool and hip than Mom or Dad), and they might defy it. But ask any twentysomething if it's likely they will grow up to look like Mom and Dad, and you won't get defiance. You'll just get a nod.

By the time we become parents ourselves it's a settled fact—*we are our parents*. We hear ourselves saying to our kids the same things our parents said to us. We find ourselves drifting toward our parents' patterns of spending or their view of the world, and soon enough we might even start dressing like them. At some point wearing dress socks with tennis shoes like Dad used to doesn't seem like such a crazy idea after all.

My wife, Shelley, tells me all the time that a gesture of mine is just like "Big Lou's." She'll say that the way I smirked or the way I cut my eyes or the way I said what I said was just like him. Or she'll say, when I respond a certain way, "Martha Jeane (my mom), is that you?!"

But the journey to becoming like our parents doesn't just result from our genetic makeup. It also comes from watching our parents from our earliest moments of life, from modeling what we saw them do.

There's a photo of Shelley taken when she was a little girl that I absolutely love. She's standing next to her dad during a family vacation. I think her mom must have taken the photo because she's not in it. Shelley's maybe four years old, and she and her dad are by the side of the road at one of those scenic overlooks where you pull over your car and get out and look around. Snowcapped mountains are behind them, and Shelley and her dad are standing about two feet away from the edge of a cliff. There's no guardrail on the cliff, just a little berm of stacked rocks, and Shelley's wearing a white sweater with outrageous black-and-white checked pants, flared. Her dad has on a late 1960s-era jacket and slacks, his legs are flexed like he might need to make a move really fast, and he's got his hand on Shelley's shoulder like he doesn't feel completely comfortable with the whole setup because they're so close to the edge. One of the best parts of the whole image is that both Shelley and her dad are wearing cool-cat sunglasses. Shelley's sunglasses are just about the same size as her dad's, and you can almost hear the exuberance in her voice that day: *Yessir, I'm wearing shades too. Just like my dad!*

Do you have any favorite pictures of you with your dad? If you don't, that's okay; we're walking through this slowly. We're breathing in the truth that God is our perfect Father, constantly shifting our eyes off of us and onto Jesus, who reveals Abba God to us.

I'm pointing us to pictures because when I look at that picture of Shelley and her dad, I see a lot of family love, for sure. But what I also see is some big-time modeling. You know how when you're a kid and you look up at your father and you do the things he's doing? Sometimes you even wear what he's wearing, especially sunglasses. That's happening in this snapshot. All of us are the products of our DNA and of what was modeled for us.

Shelley's not alone when it comes to wanting to do what her dad was doing when she was a kid; there's another family picture we bring out every so often for laughs. This one's of me. I'm slightly younger, maybe two. It's Atlanta, Georgia, circa 1960, during one of the not-so-frequent winter snows. I'm standing next to a snowman that my dad built, but man, it's no ordinary snowman. I told you my dad was crazy-talented in art and design and unique when it came to seeing the world. Now, any old snowman is three big snowballs stacked on top of each other with sticks for arms, rocks for a mouth and eyes, and a carrot nose. But no, not this snowman.

This snowman looks like a marble statue. He's five feet

tall and made of perfectly polished snow. His arms flawlessly contour into the body so his hands are clasped in front. His face looks like a carved bust of Tumnus, the impish faun from C. S. Lewis's *The Lion, the Witch, and the Wardrobe*. I guarantee there's not another dad in the whole city of Atlanta who ever built his kids a snowman like *that*.

This is a big reason I've spent my whole life doing things differently, a little off the beaten path. When I was little and I first saw that snowman, that freaky thing is what I thought was normal! But mainly, I saw Dad's work, and I wanted to do things just like Dad.

We all copy the behaviors and heart attitudes of our fathers, right? And later in life, for good or bad, we must all confront what we've grown to emulate. If your dad loved to drive 42 miles per hour in the fast lane on the freeway, then chances are there are cars regularly zooming around you when you drive. We can't make this stuff up. We all saw characteristics, mannerisms, reactions, and patterns in our earthly fathers, and plenty of those behaviors and attitudes found their way into our lives too. Teenagers, believe what you will, but the power of DNA is strong. And modeling, in fact, does mold us.

New Building Blocks

Here's a twist—in Christ you have been born twice, so you have a new Father to resemble, and there's a whole new heritage stream coming down to you. That means, as we've talked about already, you have two family trees. It also means you have two birth certificates. One is earthly, one heavenly. On one is the date and place you entered this world. On the other is the date and place you put your faith in Jesus as Savior and Lord of your life. In the case of the latter, that's the moment God brought you from spiritual death to life through your faith in the finished work of Jesus on the cross. Your spiritual birth certificate announces that you were born again, that you are now and forever a son or a daughter of God.

We see this in John's gospel where he described our new birth this way: "Yet to all who did receive [Jesus], to those who believed in his name, he gave the right to become children of God—children born not of natural descent, nor of human decision or a husband's will, but born of God" (John 1:12–13).

You may feel you aren't good enough to earn God's love and to deserve a place in His family. Or you may be striving, hoping your good deeds outweigh the bad and land you in heaven one day. But forget that. It's hopeless. And God isn't counting your sins anymore because He already laid them on His innocent Son when He died in your place on the cross.

See, the power of the gospel message is this: Sin doesn't make you a bad person. No, it's much worse than that. Sin makes you a spiritually dead person. "The wages [result] of sin is death" (Romans 6:23). And being dead is a major problem because dead people can't do a thing to help themselves.

That's why what God has done for us is called *good news*! Jesus didn't leave heaven and die on a cross to make bad people better people. He gave His life as a sacrifice for our sin and rose again so He could bring us from death to life. The verse continues: ". . . but the gift of God is eternal life in Christ Jesus our Lord" (Romans 6:23).

God's love set a rescue plan in place for you not because you deserved or earned it but because of His great love for you. "See what great love the Father has lavished on us, that we should be called children of God! And that is what we are!" (1 John 3:1). That's what we are because we have been born again as sons and daughters of God.

God's love is described here as *lavish*. It's not paper-thin or dirt cheap. His love is not flimsy or silver-plated. It's solid gold. And there's enough of His love for every moment—for all your highs and lows in life—and for every circumstance you'll ever face.

I love how Eugene Peterson describes God's love in his version of Psalm 36: "God's love is meteoric, his loyalty astronomic, his purpose titanic, his verdicts oceanic. Yet in his largeness nothing gets lost; not a man, not a mouse, slips through the cracks. How exquisite your love, O God!" (vv. 5–7 MSG).

There's something more profound than just having a new spiritual birth certificate. You also now have the spiritual DNA of God. When you were born physically, everything you got came from your earthly parents. But your spiritual birth isn't about getting anything at all from your mom and dad. They may have influenced you in your faith, encouraged you in your understanding of Jesus, and shown you what it looked like to follow Him. But when you were born again, everything you received in the new you, you got from God.

Look again at how this came to be: we are "children born not of natural descent, nor of human decision or a husband's will, but born of God" (John 1:12–13). God is our perfect heavenly Father. And we are born of God. That means we have new spiritual DNA coursing through us. God's DNA. Sure, I still have my DNA from Louie my dad and Martha Jeane my mom, and I received some character traits and physiology from them. But praise God, He is giving me new life. I am born again by the Spirit of God, so that means I have received a brand-new spiritual DNA from God. If you have received Him and believe in His name, then you also possess this new DNA. This spiritual DNA brings new dimensions of structure for your character, for your coping mechanisms, for your patterned responses—new building blocks for your very soul.

When we receive this new spiritual DNA, it means whole new possibilities open up. Romans 6:6–13 indicates that our old nature was crucified right along with Jesus on the cross so that our old selves ruled by sin might be done away with. Our parental natural DNA is still part of us, but thanks to Christ, we are no longer bound by our old sinful nature. We are not slaves to sin anymore. Jesus has set us free from sin, and we are alive to God in Jesus Christ. Second Corinthians 5:17 calls us "new creations."

That doesn't mean we become divine. We're not "little gods," and we're not equal to God in any way. Yet the Bible says a new nature has been given to us by God. We actually have the Spirit of Jesus living inside of us (2 Corinthians 13:5). Paul said, "It is no longer I who live, but Christ who lives in me" (Galatians 2:20 ESV), and Paul further described how Christ can "make his home in [our] hearts" through faith (Ephesians 3:17 NLT).

That's fantastic news for you and me because it means the domino effect of our human DNA, those particular characteristics that constitute the sin nature, can be broken by the power of the life and death and resurrection of the Son of the living God. The old has passed away. A new life has begun. We are sons and daughters of God. Everything has changed.

Stopping the Trickle-Down Effect

There's one more thing that results from your new birth that's a game changer for your future. You are no longer a slave to the behavior you have seen modeled by your father (or mother). You are not a slave to the sins of your father. In

You are a

uniquely
designed,
wonderfully
created,
dearly loved
child of a
perfect
Father.

Christ, you have the spiritual DNA of almighty God woven into your soul. That means you *are free* to do what you see your heavenly Father doing.

No matter what kind of relationship you had with your earthly father, if you are left to operate only out of your natural DNA, you're never going to reach your full potential as a child of God. Sure, you'll have the advantage of the good traits of your parents, but you'll also suffer the downstream consequences of their genetic and behavioral flaws.

If you're a daughter who never got a loving embrace from your dad, it's possible that you've sought to find that embrace in the arms of a lot of other men. If you're a son who watched your dad struggle with rage or the bottle or porn or unfaithfulness or greed or aimlessness, it's likely you swore at some point you'd never be like him in that way. Yet, years later, you see the seeds of his faults trying to take root in the soil of your life.

The ripple effects of sin are strong, and the consequences of our actions don't impact just our own lives. Dads, there's a lot riding on your choices and the patterns you develop. You're not just modeling attitudes and behavior for your children; you are passing on to them the sin patterns that you think they may not see. "The LORD is slow to anger, abounding in love and forgiving sin and rebellion. Yet he does not leave the guilty unpunished; he punishes the children for the sin of the parents to the third and fourth generation" (Numbers 14:18). This doesn't mean you are going to have to give account for your father's sinful choices. And it doesn't mean that God is eager to dump on you something your father did (or does). The Lord is not like that. He is slow to anger and He overflows with love and forgiveness. But sin has a trickle-down effect, corrupting generations to come.

The King James Version, and several other versions of the Bible, translates the last phrase of Numbers 14:18 as, ". . . visiting the iniquity of the fathers upon the children unto the third and fourth generation." The word *visiting* in this verse has a simple and clear meaning—that the father's sins have a way of showing up in the lives of their kids. Sometimes the visit comes a day later, and at other times, ten years down the road. But at some point it's likely there's going to be a knock at the door, and Dad's sin is going to be looking to stay for a while.

For example, my dad was an Olympic-caliber, gold medal–winning worrier. So, naturally, I can be prone to worry. Just saying I'll never be like him won't work. And that's just the tip of the iceberg. His depression has come calling. His loneliness has rung my doorbell more than a few times.

In saying this I'm not encouraging you or me to blame what's wrong with us on our dads, or on anyone for that matter. That approach to freedom doesn't work. I'm simply saying that, like it or not, the attitudes, actions, tendencies, shortcomings, and outright rebellious, sinful choices of our dads are doing their best right now to set up shop and get control of our lives.

But here's the key.

Dwelling on the negatives we have seen in our earthly

fathers only serves to reinforce the behaviors or patterns that we *don't want* in our lives. Every time you play that old tape of what your dad did, swearing up and down that you'll never do anything like that, you are rehearsing once again the very thing you are trying not to do!

I'm not going to be a workaholic. I'm not going to be a workaholic. I am not going to be a workaholic. I am not going to be a workaholic. I am not going to be a workaholic. When you say that, you just get "workaholic" ingrained five more times in your psyche. You underscore five more times what you don't want to become.

If we're not careful, the opposite effect can also happen. We declare: *I'll never talk to my kids that way.* Or *I'll never raise my voice like that.* Or *I'll never lose control in anger.*

And we don't. But because we have camped out on the negative things that we don't want to become for so long, we end up swinging to the far opposite edge in our parenting style. We never discipline our children, create healthy boundaries, or enforce consequences when any boundaries are willfully broken. Above all, we want our kids to like us, so we turn our promise to not be like our parents into an excuse for not being the true parent our kids desperately need. The result can be kids who can't function in a consequential world and who are not sure they are truly loved.

Sure, on the surface no child wants boundaries, but without boundaries it's possible they'll wonder if they are really valuable to their parents. So the kids are unsure about life because there were no guardrails, yet in the parent's mind they succeeded. They didn't raise their voice like their dad.

You see, fighting the negative only puts us on the wrestling mat with what we don't want to become. And it's a fight we cannot win in our flesh.

Revival on the Inside

Because that fight is impossible in our natural capacity, that's why this idea of new birth is so revolutionary! Bad habits aren't really broken as much as they are replaced by good habits. Negative thoughts don't just go away because we want them to. They go away when they are replaced by good and positive thoughts.

That's the beauty of being able to live out the potential of our new spiritual DNA. We are not left to try to dynamite the "old us" in our own strength. We have a spiritual revival happening on the inside, new spiritual genetics that are informing the way we think and live.

The new standard for our lives that we find in Ephesians 5:1 is this: "Therefore, be imitators of God, as dearly loved children" (csb). You can actually resemble the characteristics of your heavenly Father. People will begin thinking things such as, *He's sounding more and more like his Father. She has her Father's way of relating to people.* God's goal for your life does not end with spiritual birth. His plan is to watch you grow into spiritual maturity. He's thrilled that you've been born again. But His plan is for you to grow up to become a mighty woman of God, a mighty man of faith. And He knows you can or He would never have sent out this invitation.

Instead of fighting against the tide of the old ways handed down by your father, you can rehearse the new ways you see in your heavenly Father. Try saying this: *I'm going to get better at making wise decisions. I'm going to get better at making wise decisions. I'm going to get better at making wise decisions. I'm going to get better at making wise decisions. I'm going to get better at making wise decisions.* Five times you have reinforced who you *do* want to become! You are replacing the negative with a new picture of who God says you can become. Why would you want to do this? Because your Father is wise, and His truth teaches you to think like He thinks. His Spirit gives clarity and courage to make the right choice at the right time.

The most natural thing in the world is to grow up to be like your earthly father (not inevitable, as we've discussed, because bad patterns can be broken). But just as little children grow to resemble their parents, in the same way, your perfect Father wants you to get used to the idea of growing up spiritually to look like Him. It might seem like a high bar from where you're standing, but He knows it's possible for you to grow up and be like your heavenly Abba. You are free from the past and able to become who God has made you to be.

Set Free

Remember that moment when John the Baptist pulled Jesus up out of the Jordan River after Jesus' baptism and the voice was heard from heaven? The voice didn't say, *Hey, everyone, this is My slave! He's going to work really hard and do everything I need Him to do.*

No, the Father said, "This is my Son, whom I love; with him I am well pleased" (Matthew 3:17). Yes, Jesus was going to work really hard, and He was going to fulfill all the plans and purposes of His Father. But the Father wanted Him to know first and foremost He was a Son.

It's the same with you. In Christ you are no longer a slave to the old way of life; you are a daughter—a son—of the Father.

> The Spirit you received does not make you slaves, so that you live in fear again; rather, the Spirit you received brought about your adoption to sonship. And by him we cry, *"Abba*, Father." The Spirit himself testifies with our spirit that we are God's children. Now if we are children, then we are heirs—heirs of God and co-heirs with Christ, if indeed we share in his sufferings in order that we may also share in his glory. (Romans 8:15–17)

This is the benefit of God's rescue plan.

> But when the set time had fully come, God sent his Son, born of a woman, born under the law, to redeem those

under the law, that we might receive adoption to sonship. Because you are his sons, God sent the Spirit of his Son into our hearts, the Spirit who calls out, "Abba, Father." So you are no longer a slave, but God's child; and since you are his child, God has made you also an heir. (Galatians 4:4–7)

Your identity is that of a loved child. And you are free. Think about some of the ways your freedom releases you:

- You are no longer a slave to the abandonment you experienced when your dad decided he didn't want to be a part of your life anymore. It happened, but it doesn't define you.
- You are no longer a slave to fear, unsure about the future because you never knew if your dad was going to show up or not.
- You are no longer a slave to the kind of thinking that says, *None of the men in our family have been faithful to their wives, and I'm scared I'm going to be like them.* Or, *My dad never showed me what a good man loving a woman looked like and I'm afraid I'm never going to be able to find the right one because I don't know what I'm supposed to be looking for.*
- You are no longer a slave to the wall you've erected to protect your heart from additional hurt in the event your dad didn't call, or show up, or reach out, or care.

- You are no longer a slave to divorce. It's real and you live in its wake every day, but it doesn't dictate who you are.
- You are no longer a slave to the abuse or the addiction of your parents or even the grave where your father is buried.
- You are no longer a slave to the persona or character you have created for yourself in an attempt to escape the pain of your real life; the alter ego that's just a projection to the world—you trying to convince them and yourself that you're okay.
- You are no longer a slave to the role of sole mediator and keeper of the peace between your parents, a role you may have filled since you were a small child.
- You are no longer a slave to the heart numbness you have grown accustomed to.
- You are no longer a slave to living life at an emotional distance from everyone you care about, afraid of repeating past relational failures and the pain it might bring.
- You are no longer a slave to dread, that looming sense that cancer or an accident or some other terrible fate is going to rob you of everyone you love.
- You are no longer a slave to the codependency of being what your mom needed when your dad bailed on her and the family.
- You are no longer a slave to the thinking that you'll never be good enough.

- You are no longer a slave to the lie that you're not worthy of love.
- You are no longer a slave to comparison.
- You are no longer a slave to the idea that you'll never have a father's embrace.

You, my friend, are a uniquely designed, wonderfully created, dearly loved son—or daughter—of a perfect Father. And "There is no fear in love, but perfect love casts out fear" (1 John 4:18 ESV).

All this is yours because through Christ you were born again. Born as a child of God with new spiritual genes!

These spiritual genes are there at your rebirth, and in the next chapter we'll look at how we grow stronger and how we become men and women who reflect our Father's heartbeat to the world.

Chapter 10

Be Imitators of God

Well-known author and pastor Tim Keller underscores how remarkable it is to have the almighty God as our Father:

> The only person who dares wake up a king at 3:00 a.m. for a glass of water is a child. We have that kind of access.[11]

At any moment you can call on your heavenly Father and He will hear you. From anywhere on earth you can approach the throne of thrones. With one breath you can be in conversation with God.

But let's look more closely at the analogy of the little child who can wake the king. It's a touching image, for sure. And such a powerful reminder of the proximity we are afforded to God. Yet, ten years later, when the child is now a teenager, do we still want the fourteen-year-old waking the king in the middle of the night? Of course not!

We, and the king, want the maturing teen to get the glass of water for themselves, right? And maybe get the king one too!

Eventually, you want that child to learn the ways of roy-alty, the manners of the household, the decision-making skills of management, the affairs of state, the decorum of the posi-tion the family has been afforded.

Fast-forward twenty years and you want to see that same child, now a man, engaging guests from other nations, hold-ing conversations with maturity and poise, and exhibiting character and actions that reflect well on the namesake of the king.

The access we have to God as loved sons and daughters is incredible. But as God's children the ultimate goal is to grow into the likeness of our heavenly Father—to grow up and reflect Him.

If the blessing of God being our Father was all there was to the relationship, then we could end this book right here. But there's more than simply receiving the blessing of being loved sons and daughters of God. At the end of the blessing comes a phenomenal opportunity and responsibility—We're invited to model our lives after our heavenly Father.

Beyond the Mushed-Up Peas

Some people never act on this incredible opportunity. *I'm fine with just the blessing of being a child, thanks.* Maybe that's the case for you. You're loved. You're accepted. God is involved in your life. So you'll take your new identity as the child of a perfect Father and sit on that identity. You are content to stay in the blissful innocence of being held like a baby in the Father's arms, someone who never takes responsibility to grow up.

I hope that's not your way of thinking. Given that you are still reading, I'm assuming you're actually energized by the prospect of maturing spiritually beyond your current state. You want to live a life that reflects the Father who has lavished you with His love. You don't want to be one of those Christians Paul wrote about in 1 Corinthians 3. Paul lamented that the believers had stayed "mere infants in Christ" (v. 1). He wanted to give them spiritual solid food, but they weren't ready for it. He could only give them milk because they were still worldly.

How sad to live in this condition. Others around you are growing and developing, but you still have the maturity of an infant.

Imagine that all your friends are going to a barbeque on the beach. You can count on there being baby back ribs, salmon on the grill, and all the best side dishes. Frisbees will be flying, and the night will be filled with laughter and stories by the fire. Your mouth is watering at the aromas coming off the grill.

But there's a problem. You don't have any teeth!

Hey bud, you have any mushed-up peas or something I can eat from a baby food jar?

How ridiculous would that be? Yet so many children of God have never grown up in their faith. They are still in spiritual infancy. Can't walk. Can't chew solid food. Can't withstand high winds of adversity. Don't know God's Word. Can't help someone else grow stronger in their faith.

It's great when we fully own the initial blessing of knowing God as our perfect Father. But then we are offered the additional blessing and opportunity of growing up to look and act like our heavenly Father. If we simply stay at the level of the first blessing, then our lives stagnate. We miss out on the blessings of becoming spiritual adults and tapping into all the potential that is woven into us at the moment of spiritual birth.

Earlier we cracked open the first verse of Ephesians 5, but let's look at it more deeply and keep reading. "Therefore be imitators of God, as dearly loved children, and walk in love, as Christ also loved us and gave himself up for us, a sacrificial and fragrant offering to God" (vv. 1–2, csb).

Be imitators of God. Just let those words sink in. That means we are to follow God's example. We are to do what God does. We're to think what God thinks. We're to care how God cares. We're to place our feet in His footsteps. We're to imitate God our perfect heavenly Father the same way children imitate their earthly fathers. We have a responsibility and an opportunity to grow up and look and act like God.

Think about it from God's perspective. God is saying to us, "I want you to continually shape your life in such a way that you look like Me, sound like Me, talk like Me, act like Me, and think like Me, more and more."

Be Imitators of Abba Father

Maybe at first take you're thinking this is impossible—imitating the divine—but imitating God is not out of reach for us. God isn't cruel. He's not throwing down a monumental challenge that we can never rise to while He sits back and laughs at us, knowing we'll never be able to accomplish that goal. No. God has something far greater in mind. Look closely at the end of verse two. God says, "Be imitators of God, as dearly loved children, *and walk in love, as Christ also loved us*" (emphasis added).

Notice the progression in Ephesians 5:1–2. We start our spiritual growth by knowing we are dearly loved children—and then we move on from there and live a life of love. And it's not just any old love; it's getting into the rhythm of loving the same way Christ loved us. Our modeling after God is not based on our behavior. He bases the foundation of our spiritual change on our identity as beloved children of God.

In verse 1, the words *dearly loved* are identity words for us, words to rest in and soak ourselves in every day of our lives. We are *dearly loved* children! And once we have our new identity in mind, we are to "walk in love, as Christ loved us." That means we are to imitate God by doing what Jesus did. We don't start imitating God by deciding one day we're going to become more spiritual. We don't start imitating God by reading a book of character traits and trying to hammer our habits into new shapes. We start imitating God by knowing we're born spiritually into a new relationship with God, where we know we're the beloved children of God. From there, we look to Jesus. We live a life of love just like Jesus loves us. And, having received His love, we seek to reflect that love to others.

To reflect God by loving others is at the core of spiritual maturity. Colossians 3:14 talks about how we need to "put on love" almost like it's a jacket to be worn, and let me tell you, the garment of love works for every event we ever need to show up for. It's for office use and daily use and weekend use and evening use. We can sleep in it. We can celebrate in it. We can work out in it. We can get married in it. The garment of love is all-purpose, and the garment of love is ready to wear.

Then we let this love "guide [our] life" (TLB), or "[bind] everything together in perfect harmony" (ESV). So say somebody is in your life, and that person is really hard to love. If you don't know God, then it's easy to push that person aside. You conclude that the person is a jerk, and while you might be outwardly polite to the person (or maybe not), you don't feel a responsibility to love jerks. If you're a Jesus follower, however, then you're called to love that person, and that calling can feel difficult to live out.

The key to maturity isn't that you summon the effort by yourself and try really hard to love the person that's tough to love (or even to like). The key is to remember your new identity as a dearly loved child of God, and then proceed from there. God loved you first, even when you didn't deserve it, even when you might have been a first-class jerk. And because you are loved by God, you can let God's love flow through you and out from you to anyone who's in your life. You aren't going to hoard the love of God. You're going to release it.

Becoming a Channel of His Love

Early on we introduced the image of standing under a waterfall of God's love. Let's dwell on that a little longer. Imagine the love of God pouring down on you from a huge elevated river source. You're standing at the foot of a waterfall. It's the biggest waterfall you've ever seen. You're drinking in this love. You're being washed and made new by this love. Then the love that goes out from you is like a pipeline that carries the water from you to all the people in your life. You're vitally connected to the river source, and you simply let the water flow from the source to the other person.

You start walking with a new mindset: *There's joy, compassion, humility, and patience flowing into my life so fast and abundantly that I can't even try to stop it. All I'm going to do is hold my hands above my head and worship the God who is sending this waterfall of love. I could never contain it or keep this goodness for myself. I want to spread this same love to people everywhere I go.*

It's been said that hurt people hurt people. But it's also true that loved people love people. Accepted people accept people. And blessed people bless people.

This is why it's so important to stay under the flow of the waterfall that's crashing down on you. Negative feelings and thoughts from the past can easily creep back into your heart and mind. Old ways of believing about your worth and significance can resurface. The Enemy isn't going to let you waltz into this new way of life without a fight. He's going to try to take you back to the places of hurt and disappointment over and over. He's going to try to convince you that you don't matter to people and you don't matter to God.

If the devil succeeds in getting you to revert to old views, he can stop the flow of God's abundant blessing. No, he can't stop God from loving you, but he can stop you from basking in that love and reflecting it to those around you. That's why it's so important for you to continually upgrade your thinking so it reflects God's truth.

Off with the Old, On with the New

Did you notice that Ephesians 5 begins with the word "therefore," a word that always relates back to something stated earlier? In this case, "therefore" refers to the encouragement Paul gave in the previous chapter. There, we are taught "to put off [our] old self, which is being corrupted by its deceitful desires; to be made new in the attitudes of [our] minds; and to put on the new self, created to be like God in true righteousness and holiness" (4:22–24).

That "old self," the one we are to put off, is who we

were before we started following Jesus. Our old self is bent toward destruction. It loves to be selfish and lustful and rageful and impatient. The old self is guided by our earthly desires that falsely promise to lead us toward goodness but actually lead us toward evil. So it's like Paul was saying, *Hey, do you want to become mature? Then you must realize you have a new identity. You're a dearly loved child of God now. Throw away your old identity, the one that hurt you, and start living out of your new identity, the new self. Your new self is created to imitate God in His righteousness and holiness, in His justice and compassion.*

Did you catch that? In Christ you are "created to be like God in true righteousness and holiness." Wow! It's right there in black and white. Growing up like our perfect Father is the most natural thing we can do.

Sadly, there is a strain of teaching in the church—actually it's more like a virus—that goes like this: *We're all sinners, and sinners are gonna sin. It's who we are and what we do.*

While it's true that we all still have the capacity to sin (no one needs to be convinced of that!), we also have the capacity to follow in the footsteps of our Father. We were born with a purely sinful nature. But now, in Christ, everything has changed. We are not identified any longer simply as *sinners*. We are God's children, created *to be like God* in righteousness (right things) and holiness (God-honoring things). In Christ we are made righteous, holy, and new.

As such, your Father is leading you to change the way you think! To put off the old and put on the new. Living this new way is your opportunity and responsibility. That's how you grow up so that you can stop eating mushed-up peas and start eating grilled steak.

The phrase in Ephesians 4, "be made new in the attitude of your minds," is key, because our transformation toward spiritual maturity happens not only in our hearts but in our minds too. Being made new is ultimately the work of the Holy Spirit in our lives, yet we have the responsibility to partner with the Holy Spirit in this transforming work. Our responsibility is to deliberately feed new thoughts into our minds. We become good thinkers—and I don't mean we need to be super brainy. I mean we must plow and weed our minds like the soil of a healthy field is plowed and weeded.

Maybe we're prone to lustful thoughts in our heads, or angry thoughts, or downcast thoughts. That's our old self at work. To become spiritually mature, we have to soak our minds constantly in the truths of Scripture. First Peter 1:13 tells us to "[prepare] our minds for action" (ESV). Psalm 101:3 encourages us to "set no worthless thing before [our] eyes" (NASB). Philippians 4:8 challenges us to constantly dwell on thoughts that are true, honorable, right, pure, lovely, excellent, and admirable. Isaiah 26:3 promises peace to those people whose minds are steadfastly fixed on God.

So the case is logical. We imitate God by first understanding that our identity is changed, and we are now children of a perfect Father. We learn to imitate God by receiving the love of Christ into our lives and then letting this love flow through us to other people. We grow in learning how to reflect God by putting off our old self that's corrupted by things that harm us and by putting on our new self.

Embracing our identity as a "new self" is key. As we talked about earlier, when we are saved through faith in Jesus, we are given a new spiritual DNA. Our spirit is awakened to a new kind of life. We are born again. And since we are children born of God, we have God's spiritual DNA now. Again, that doesn't mean we become "little gods." It means we have God's life inside of us. We imitate God by becoming the mouth of God, the eyes of God, the ears of God, the hands of God, the feet of God, the heart of God, the thoughts of God, the compassion of God, the justice of God, the love of God. That's how we mature. That's how we grow up.

Remember the aunt who showed up at Thanksgiving and declared we were starting to look like Mom or Dad? A similar sort of thing happens in our spiritual lives. Old habits fade away and are replaced by good ones. We learn to set harmful things aside. We learn to embrace helpful things that are good for us. Pretty soon someone comes to our front door, someone we haven't seen in a while. That person is around us for a while and can't help but exclaim: *Man, you've changed so much. You're not as angry as you used to be. You seem less depressed. You're not drinking like you used to.*

Eventually, we hope they will say, *Wow, you've grown spiritually. You're starting to look just like your heavenly Father!*

God has spanned
heaven and earth

to
reach
you.

Participate in the Divine

This process of maturing spiritually is often described by the word *discipleship*. That word indicates that as we become followers of Jesus, imitators of God, we become disciples of Jesus, people who stay connected to Him, who go where He goes and who do what He does. One of the central verses that points us toward this path of discipleship is 2 Peter 1:3: "His divine power has given us everything we need for a godly life through our knowledge of him who called us by his own glory and goodness."

We have everything we need for a godly life. His divine power has given us everything. Everything! Perhaps we haven't learned how to use everything to the fullest extent. But the working parts are already in place. Thanks to our new birth, Christ actually lives inside of us, as it says in Colossians 1:27: "Christ in you, the hope of glory." We have everything we need for godliness. We have Christ!

We read further in 2 Peter 1:4, "Through these he has given us his very great and precious promises, so that through them you may participate in the divine nature, having escaped the corruption in the world caused by evil desires."

Wow! Look at that phrase—we "may participate in the divine nature." This is our new spiritual DNA at work. Thanks to our spiritual birth, we can share in God's divine nature. We possess a new spiritual genetic makeup within us. That helps set us on the road to being imitators of God, because the life of God is flowing through us. Jesus is a "life-giving spirit" (1 Corinthians 15:45). The Holy Spirit changes our hearts (Romans 2:29). We are made alive with Christ (Ephesians 2:4–5), and because of Christ, "now we really live" (1 Thessalonians 3:8).

Is this becoming clear to you? It may be easier to think of the process of discipleship in steps, even though discipleship is not so much a step-by-step process as it is a relationship lived out in real time. As we walk with God, God shows us how to truly live. Yet for those of us who like things laid out, let me offer three markers on the road to spiritual maturity. Three steps in the pathway of discipleship. As we imitate God, as we grow up to be like our heavenly Father, these are the markers we're looking for. These are the things we should expect to see in our lives. Conveniently, all three of these markers begin with the letter *A*.

1. We Awaken

We awaken to *who* we are and to *whose* we are. The more spiritually mature we become, the more we constantly remind ourselves of the truth of our new identity. We are not merely followers of beliefs about God; we have a new essence thanks to our new relationship with God. He is our perfect heavenly Father, and we are His beloved children.

That's our identity!

Our understanding of our new identity changes everything for us. By nature, we are not lost spiritual pilgrims. We are not simply churchgoers. We are not trying to be do-gooders. We are not merely shined-up sinners. Who we are now at the core is this: We are born of God. He is our perfect Father. We have received Christ, and we believe in His name. We lean in to the truth that Jesus Christ is the sacrifice for our sins. He is the Savior of the world, the life giver, the life healer, the life changer, the deliverer, and the redeemer. With an understanding of this new identity, we are given the opportunity and responsibility of growing up to look like our heavenly Father. We must constantly remind ourselves of our new nature, our new DNA. The further we get in our Christian walk, the more we look and act and sound like our heavenly Father.

It's like waking up after being asleep, where we wandered around in a nightmare of lostness. The more we awaken to who we are and to whose we are, the more we constantly watch our Father. We listen to Him. We observe Him at work. Why? Because in our wide-awake new life we want to live like Him. And as we're imitating our Father, He's constantly shaping and teaching us. It's a two-way street. God participates in our lives. He's saying, "Here, let Me show you how to do that." He's showing us how to be imitators of Him.

2. We Accept

The second marker of spiritual maturity is that we accept the implications and possibilities of our new genetic makeup. It's one thing to believe in Jesus, to acknowledge that God is our perfect heavenly Father and that we're beloved children of God, and it's another thing to truly live out those realities.

If we're truly living in light of our new identity, then our lives will change, and we will lean toward that change in conjunction with the power of the Holy Spirit working inside of us. By grace, we will deliberately walk that new direction with our minds and hearts and wills and whole beings. We put off the old man and put on the new man, and we won't tolerate the stink of sin in our lives anymore.

Far too often, even though we're believers, we develop a comfortable tolerance of our old ways. We walk in fear or shame or unconfessed sin, and we just stay that way. But as dearly loved children of God, it's up to us to shout, *Enough!* to the old ways of living. By faith, we can claim the light of Christ to guide our pathways. We must not settle for second-rate living anymore. We want to truly live, in Jesus' name. So, we "throw off everything that hinders and the sin that so easily entangles. And [we] run with perseverance the race marked out for us, fixing our eyes on Jesus" (Hebrews 12:1–2).

In time, we learn to do nothing apart from Christ (John 15:5). We abide in Him; we dwell in Him; we stay close to Him, because we learn that if we don't, then our lives are a mess. We learn that God has given us unlimited resources, as Peter told us—everything we need for life and godliness. In Him, we are enriched in every way (1 Corinthians 1:4–5), and thanks to God, we are blessed abundantly, "so that in all things at all times, having all that [we] need, [we] will abound in every good work" (2 Corinthians 9:8). We simply accept the bounty.

3. We Adopt

The third marker of spiritual maturity is that we're called to adopt the behavior and character of God. We model after Him. This means we pattern after Him, copy Him, emulate Him, shadow Him, echo Him, mirror Him. We model after Him and model after Him again. When an actor is getting ready to play the part of a historical figure, they study that figure—how they moved, how they gestured, their expressions, their values. They look at any film footage that may exist of that figure. They read everything that they ever wrote. Through the close relationship we have with God through Christ, we constantly study how God works and moves, and then we study Him some more. The change doesn't happen all at once. It happens bit by bit through the trueness of our walk with Him.

This progression actually takes pressure off of us, knowing our lives are transformed bit by bit. We don't learn from our earthly fathers all at once, and our heavenly Father doesn't expect us to figure everything out immediately either. In our spiritual walks, we "grow in the grace and knowledge of our Lord and Savior Jesus Christ" (2 Peter 3:18). The key word is *grow*. And growth is gradual.

Likewise, Paul told us to "be diligent in these matters; give [ourselves] wholly to them, so that everyone may see [our] progress" (1 Timothy 4:15). The key word there is *progress*. As we diligently become imitators of God, we give ourselves wholeheartedly to the possibilities of our new genetic makeup; we genuinely develop in our spiritual maturity. We move forward.

The writer of Hebrews encouraged us to "move beyond the elementary teachings about Christ and be taken forward to maturity" (Hebrews 6:1). This implies a steady and deliberate spiritual maturity. Not an immediate maturity but a definite and gradual growth.

James talks about how a tested faith produces perseverance, and how perseverance must "finish its work so that [we] may be mature and complete, not lacking anything" (James 1:4). Again, that passage implies a process that doesn't happen all at once. We observe. We practice. We make mistakes, get up, brush ourselves off, and keep going.

There's one more family photo I'd like to share with you. It's me with my dad at Fort Walton Beach, Florida, on vacation. Dad and I are both holding fish we (he) caught, and we are a mirror image of each other. I'm maybe ten years old and wearing my favorite football jersey and swim trunks; yet what's particularly interesting to me is how Dad and I are standing the same way. We're holding the fish the same way. Everything about our postures is identical, except that he's clearly my dad, and I'm clearly his son.

The funny thing is nobody told us to pose that way for the picture. Whoever was holding the camera just said, "Hey, let's get a picture of you guys and the fish you just caught" or something like that, and we both just struck the same pose automatically.

There's so much good imitating wrapped up in that picture. Sure, the process of learning how to fish was taking time. Dad needed to show me how to bait a hook, where to throw the line, how to cast, how to reel it in. And then he had to patiently untangle the line after I got it all tangled up again. I can't tell you how many times my dad and I had been fishing together before that single photograph was taken. Gradually, I was learning how to imitate my dad, little by little, day in and day out. Dad was committed to teaching me, and I was committed to learning from him.

With our spiritual lives, that photograph is a great reminder of the process of discipleship at work. Our heavenly Father teaches us to discover who we are in Him. He is our perfect Father, and we are His beloved children. The process starts at our birth, our new birth. And then little by little, bit by bit, we grow into the very likeness of God.

I don't know what kind of earthly father you had, but I know that God has spanned heaven and earth to reach you. And I know if you want one, the reality of a perfect Father can be yours. I pray your eyes are open to see Him as He truly is, and your heart is beating fast knowing His eyes arc on you and His heart is for you. His blessing is full and free. The waterfall is pouring down goodness today. His spiritual genes have re-created you and His hand is there to lead you. You can take your next step as a loved daughter—a loved son—of the perfect Father.

Your New Story Has Just Begun

As we come to the close of this book, I pray that you are sensing a shift in your view of God and that with new spiritual eyes you are seeing you are not abandoned and never will be. Seeing God as a trustworthy and good Father, the perfect Father you've always longed for. And I hope that you're seeing this book as a "letter from heaven," reaching you right where you are with a promise of a brand-new way of life.

You might be thinking, *I wish I'd heard this truth years ago. It would have changed my life.*

But the beauty is you're hearing it now, and your life is changing as the love of God explodes in your heart, tearing down walls you built to protect yourself and building up confidence and faith in a God who is for you. A God who will not leave you behind.

Do you remember Thomas, the disciple of Jesus? He was

part of Jesus' inner circle as He performed miracles, gave amazing teachings, and moved from town to town, inviting people into the kingdom of God. If you do remember Thomas, it's likely that your first thought about him is that he's the one known as "Doubting Thomas."

If you haven't heard of Thomas, he gets that description because he missed out on the moment when Jesus appeared to the disciples after His resurrection. On that momentous occasion Thomas wasn't present. When told about what had transpired—that Jesus showed up and showed them all the scars in His hands and side from His crucifixion—Thomas didn't believe it. Maybe Thomas was frustrated that he missed it, having the ultimate case of FOMO. Or perhaps he was like some of us—he needed more evidence before he could confidently assert that Jesus was alive.

Whatever the case, Jesus was not going to leave Thomas behind. On a second occasion Jesus appeared to the same group in the same place. But this time Thomas was there.

> A week later his disciples were in the house again, and Thomas was with them. Though the doors were locked, Jesus came and stood among them and said, "Peace be with you!" Then he said to Thomas, "Put your finger here; see my hands. Reach out your hand and put it into my side. Stop doubting and believe." Thomas said to him, "My Lord and my God!" Then Jesus told him, "Because you have seen me, you have believed; blessed are those who have not seen and yet have believed." (John 20:26–29)

Two things jump out to me as I read about this encounter between Jesus and Thomas. One, Jesus came back a second time. Jesus didn't say at His first appearance, *Well, it's too bad My buddy Thomas isn't here. Knowing him, he'll need the facts and will have a hard time simply believing I'm alive based on what you guys say. What a shame, he'll probably get left behind.* Nope. Jesus wanted Thomas to be in His resurrection story, so He managed to arrange another visit when He knew Thomas would be there.

The other thing that stands out from this meeting between Jesus and Thomas is Jesus' invitation—"Put your finger here; see my hands." Jesus was inviting Thomas to put his finger into the very scar where the nails had been driven through His body days before. Jesus knew that for Thomas to move forward he needed to stop pressing in on his doubt and start pressing in on Jesus' scars, on the place where He was wounded for all of us.

In the same way, you have now discovered that God wants to be your perfect Father and He doesn't want to move on without you. And you've seen that He will heal your wounds as you link your freedom to the healed wounds of Jesus.

I realize God's work of restoration takes time, and I am aware that things between you and your dad might not change for the better. But there's no going back. You are loved and you know it. You are free, and there's nothing to fear. God has started a new work in your heart, and He's not stopping now.

I know I've shared a lot of stories about my relationship with my dad in this book, but allow me to share one more thing. It's this: while life with my dad was far from perfect, I do know he was proud of me.

A few years into his disability, and over a decade after that awkward conversation at the kitchen stove when I told my dad I was going to be a preacher, something powerful happened. Shelley and I were living in Texas, but I'd been asked to speak at my home church, First Baptist in Atlanta—on Father's Day, no less.

In many ways that opportunity was the fulfillment of my calling all those years back. On the Sunday night I shared with the church my response to God's call on my life, I walked down the aisle in that same church building. My dad wasn't there that night, but he did come this Father's Day morning.

Mom had him looking sharp, as usual, and his wheelchair was parked beside her at the end of a pew about eight rows back and just under the balcony overhang that wrapped around the sanctuary. I was nervous, as you can imagine, preaching for the legendary Charles Stanley—and in front of several thousand people. Plus, "Big Lou" was in the crowd. He'd never heard me speak in any setting before, so it was a big deal.

I didn't look his direction a lot during my message, but I was so happy he was there. And did I mention I was *nervous?* Interestingly, I was preaching a message similar to this book—about God being a perfect Father. I got through the message and at the end of the service stood near the front and shook some hands as people began to drift from the sanctuary.

Most everyone told me I did a good job and that they were
glad to have me back.

Then I saw my dad. He and Mom had been surrounded
by people, too, especially given she was a pillar in the church
before vanishing into the shadows as a full-time caregiver
for Dad, and my dad hadn't been through the doors since
long before the onset of his illness. I walked over to them and
my dad reached up to shake my hand. He was looking at me
with his piercing blue eyes and he flashed that grin of his that
would make anyone feel like a million bucks.

I think I managed to say, "I'm so glad you came," even
though I was more than a little choked up with emotion.

"Are you kidding, Ace?!" he said. "That was the best thing
I've ever heard!"

My heart was in my throat.

I knew he wasn't just being kind. I could tell he really
meant it. Dad saw the gift God had put inside me. He saw
me doing the thing that sets my heart on fire. He could
sense the work of God through the words I was sharing. And
I'm guessing that for a moment he sensed that there was a
Father above who wasn't just a bigger version of the one who
had walked out on him but a real, true, perfect Father who
cared for him.

All the hurt of our uncomfortable kitchen dance evap-
orated, and I felt my dad's blessing on me and my calling.
God had won. He chalked up a victory that day. His promise
to restore fathers and their children was actually happening
in real time. As a result, even though he has been gone for

decades, I know my dad is proud of me, even as a preacher, and I carry that affirmation with me to this day. Our story didn't end up with my dad having a radical conversion experience. But thank God there was still time for him to bless me and for me to bless him.

I realize a defining moment of receiving your earthly dad's blessing is not possible for everyone. Yet I am confident God is going to put people in your life who will affirm that what He has been teaching you about Himself is true. That's not to say we need somebody else to validate God's Word. We don't. But God has a way of using the body of Christ, the church all around us, to help us come to know the fullness of His love. Paul wrote:

> For this reason I kneel before the Father, from whom every family in heaven and on earth derives its name. I pray that out of his glorious riches he may strengthen you with power through his Spirit in your inner being, so that Christ may dwell in your hearts through faith. And I pray that you, being rooted and established in love, may have power, together with all the Lord's holy people, to grasp how wide and long and high and deep is the love of Christ, and to know this love that surpasses knowledge—that you may be filled to the measure of all the fullness of God. (Ephesians 3:14–19)

Maybe your earthly dad is not stepping in with a miraculous change of heart and a desire to bless you. Or maybe he wants to but doesn't quite know how. Either way, God is able to fill in the gaps left by our earthly dads.

Remember, God is the One who gives back what the Enemy has stolen. He is restoring what's been lost and orchestrating for you a story of overcoming grace. Surely somewhere around you He's placed a messenger in His body with a "letter from heaven" reminding you that your heavenly Father loves you, cherishes you, and will never turn His back on you.

I'm not suggesting that an envelope with a postage stamp stuck on the back is going to float down from the sky but rather that God has a way of putting people in our lives as tangible expressions of His love. Even if He didn't, we still have enough truth about His blessing to live free as His sons and daughters. But it's likely there is a friend, family member, coach, teacher, or coworker who is reflecting God's love your way. Oftentimes that person is God's instrument to encourage you to keep your eyes on Him and to never give up on His promises—to always remember your new identity in Christ and to stay anchored in His Word.

To that end—the end of you never forgetting who you have become in Christ—I have stopped and prayed for you time and time again. Every other day as I've been writing this book something has been mentioned to me or a story has been told to me, confirming that this perfect Father message is the one God wants me to share right now. I know God is doing all He can to get the message of His blessing to you. But your adversary, the devil, is working hard as well—trying to keep you broken-down and hopeless and alone. So I've been praying and writing and praying some more.

And then God dropped an *actual letter* into my hands that let me know once again that He is in the mix and that this book is landing in the right hands on the right day.

Coming down to the last few days before the manuscript for this book was due, I was preparing to share a condensed, one-talk version of what I've written in these pages during the opening session of our annual Passion Conference. My heart was already tender toward the message of fatherhood given that for the past year I'd been writing the words in these pages about my memories of my dad. That process was stirring up lots of thoughts about my family tree and the realization that I know far too little about it.

My desire to know more about my origins and my family was highlighted even more a few weeks before the moment I'm telling you about (the day I was preparing my talk for Passion), when my dad's first cousin Bobby died and I was asked to speak at the memorial service. Though we had not been particularly close, I was honored to share at his funeral, which was attended by about four dozen people, some Giglios, some not. I left the cemetery that day determined to know more about my father's father and his father.

Two weeks later I was at my desk on the afternoon before the opening session of the Passion Conference, reviewing my notes for my talk one last time. On my desk sat three unread cards and letters from various family members who had been at Bobby's memorial service. All three cards had arrived in the mail that day.

I'll open those after Passion is over, I thought, *when my mind is clear and I can read them with care.*

Then a little nudge encouraged me to read them right at that moment. One was from Bobby's son and one was from his older sister.

The last letter was from his wife, who for personal reasons could not attend the funeral service. In her note she reminded me that several years back Bobby had sent me a stack of research he had done on our family history, including information about my great-grandfather Vito who had lived and died in Atlanta.

I reread the sentence again, my eyes carefully tracing the words—"Including information about my great-grandfather Vito who had lived and died in Atlanta."

WHAT?!?!

What are you saying? I thought to myself.

My great-grandfather lived in Atlanta?!?!

Why don't I know this?

Why didn't my dad ever tell me about his grandfather Vito?

This is crazy talk!

I suddenly remembered that I had in fact received a package of photos and other memorabilia from Bobby a few years back, but it had arrived about the time we were moving and unfortunately ended up unopened in a drawer in my study. I shot up out of my chair and reached for the drawer. I found the envelope right where I thought it would be.

My heart nearly exploded over the next half hour as I went through documents and photographs and handwritten genealogies about my family. I discovered that my great-grandfather, whom I had never once heard my dad talk about, lived in my city—in Atlanta—died a mile from where I was born, and was buried twenty minutes by car from where I was sitting at my desk.

Whoa!

Add to this new revelation about my grandfather the line in her letter that underscored the reason she wanted to make sure I remembered the packet of information Bobby sent and that I knew about my great-grandfather. She wrote, "Our fathers are so very important in passing the blessing." I was stunned.

Bobby's wife didn't know I was writing this book, or wondering about my family tree, or that I was about to give a talk about the father's blessing to forty thousand eighteen-to-twenty-five-year-olds. But my heavenly Father knew all of that. And He wanted me to know He was for me. My perfect Father wanted me to be assured as I was giving the talk the next night that I was on the right track and that He was with me.

After the conference was over I made the trek to the cemetery where Vito Giglio is buried. On a small, fenced lot stood a boarded-up one-room chapel surround by a few dozen graves. Eventually I found my great-grandfather's marker. It was stark in that there were no other Giglio names to be found.

God in His kindness had linked me further into the story of my past. But then I realized something even more profound as I noticed the constant sound of jet airplanes overhead. My great-grandfather Giglio is buried in the flight pattern of the Atlanta airport, an airport I have flown in and out of hundreds of times in my life. Many of those takeoffs or landings brought me over the grave of a relative I didn't even know was there. I'd been flying over Vito's resting place without even knowing it.

Woah, again.

God wanted me to know that He was closer than I could imagine. That He had always been there.

And He's always been close to you.

Your heavenly Father knows everything you're going through. He's been there every step of the way. He's not going to end the story of your newfound "perfect Father–loved child" relationship where it's beginning today. He's going to continue to heal what's been wronged on this earth and open your eyes to see how astonishingly beautiful He is—and how loved you are by Him. Be assured, "He who began a good work in you will carry it on to completion until the day of Christ Jesus" (Philippians 1:6).

Your confidence in God doesn't need to be based on whether or not you are handed a letter like the one I received. There's enough rock-solid evidence in these pages for you to know you are loved by a perfect Father, truths rooted in the unchanging Word of our God and the finished work of Christ on the cross. Dig into His Word and keep your eyes fixed on the cross. But don't be surprised when your Father puts an unmistakable reminder in your path.

His ultimate promise is this: "I will not leave you as orphans; I will come to you" (John 14:18).

Receive it and breathe it in. Live it and reflect it to the world.

You are not forgotten.

You will never be left behind.

You are chosen.

You are dearly loved.

You are not an orphan.

You are not alone.

You are a child of God.

He knows your name.

You are His.

You are not unwanted.

You are not powerless.

You are who He says you are.

You are not defeated.

You are made new.

You have what He says you have.

You can be and do what He says you can be and do.

You are not a victim.

You are in Christ's victorious procession.

You walk side by side with the King.

You are a loved daughter of the King.

You are a loved son of the Most High.

You are a trophy of His grace.

You are the loved son or daughter of a perfect Father.

You are His light shining like a city on a hill, bringing Him glory as you grow up to be like Him.

Acknowledgments

I am so humbled to be surrounded by an amazing team of people who make it possible for you to be holding this book in your hands. As some might know, this book was previously released under the title *Not Forsaken*. Due to conditions beyond our control, that book didn't reach as wide a readership as we hoped. Given that this is a life message for me, we updated the book and are excited to rerelease it under the message's original title, *Seeing God as a Perfect Father*.

Yet this message did not originate with me. Everything we are is the result of the influence of others. The heartbeat of this book started with the teaching of one of my early mentors, Dan DeHaan. Dan modeled a passion for God that was contagious. Being around him made me want to know God more. Dan was the first person who helped me see that the Almighty was someone I could know intimately. And it was Dan who helped me realize that the God of the universe was also my Father. I've referenced Dan's book *The God You Can Know* in these pages with the hope that you'll read it for yourself. If you do, you will find the seeds of many of my core teachings and the genesis of the message in *Seeing God as a Perfect Father*.

Marcus Brotherton took my messages and shaped the

original manuscript, staying involved throughout the writing process and offering his invaluable writer's insight and skill. An accomplished author, Marcus helped translate my speaking voice to the written page as a collaborator, encourager, and friend. This book would not have come to be without his contribution.

Our team at Passion Publishing is the best. Under the skillful leadership of Kevin Marks, they support and extend the vision of the Passion Movement and of projects like this one. Kevin's willingness to partner with me is a huge reason why the message of *Seeing God as a Perfect Father* is making its way to readers around the globe.

I'm thankful for Damon Reiss and his amazing team at W Publishing. I'm humbled by Damon's belief in this book and his helpful contributions of thought that shaped the final product.

Passion's Art Director, Chandler Saunders, collaborated with the HCCP design team to help achieve the beautiful cover.

Sue Graddy and Ana Munoz lead my personal team at Passion and not only make my day-to-day life possible from a logistics point of view; they add much more in the way of wisdom, insight, and perspective to projects like this one. Their fingerprints are on this book and everything God has called me to do in this season.

Shelley and I do life together. She has been such a big encourager of this message over the years and brings the tenacity, wisdom, and discernment that make every project I undertake better. She has so much insight and leadership gold to share with the world, yet she willingly champions me and my messages in a way that is stunning and impactful. She is the most beautiful gift God has given to me.

Notes

1. Blaise Pascal, quoted in Goodreads, https://www.goodreads
   .com/quotes/801132-there-is-a-god-shaped-vacuum-in-the
   -heart-of-each.
2. Ibid.
3. Peggy Drexler, "Daughters and Dad's Approval," *Psychology Today*, June 27, 2011, https://www.psychologytoday.com/us
   /blog/our-gender-ourselves/201106/daughters-and-dads
   -approval.
4. Frank Pittman, "Fathers and Sons," *Psychology Today*,
   September 1, 1993, https://www.psychologytoday.com/us
   /articles/199309/fathers-and-sons.
5. A. W. Tozer, *The Knowledge of the Holy* (New York:
   HarperCollins, 1978), 4.
6. Tozer, *The Knowledge of the Holy*.
7. Eric Smillie, "Hubble Captures Farthest Galaxy Ever Seen,
   13.4 Billion Light Years Away," *Newsweek*, March 4, 2016,
   https://www.newsweek.com/hubble-farthest-galaxy-photo
   -video-433802.
8. Statistic according to the Census Bureau, "The Statistics
   Don't Lie: Fathers Matter," National Fatherhood Initiative,
   accessed December 24, 2022, https://www.fatherhood.org
   /father-absence-statistic.
9. "Funeral Service Transcript," *The Billy Graham Evangelistic Association*, March 2, 2018, https://memorial.billygraham.org
   /funeral-service-transcript/.

10. "People Are Better at Remembering Names Rather Than Faces," *Neuroscience News*, November 14, 2018, https://neurosciencenews.com/name-face-memory-10194; A. Mike Burton, Rob Jenkins, and David J. Robertson, "I Recognise Your Name but I Can't Remember Your Face: an Advantage for Names in Recognition Memory," *Quarterly Journal of Experimental Psychology 72, no. 7* November 14, 2018.

11. Tim Keller, Twitter post. February 23, 2015, 11:05 a.m. https://twitter.com/timkellernyc/status /569890726349307904.

About the Author

Louie Giglio is pastor of Passion City Church and original visionary of the Passion movement, which exists to call a generation to leverage their lives for the fame of Jesus.

Since 1997, Passion Conferences has gathered collegiate-aged young people in events across the US and around the world in a bold call to live for what matters most. In 2022, Passion hosted over fifty thousand students in Mercedes-Benz Stadium with another one million people joining online.

Louie is the national-bestselling author of over a dozen books, including *Don't Give the Enemy a Seat at Your Table*, *At the Table with Jesus*, *Winning the War on Worry*, *Goliath Must Fall*, *Indescribable: 100 Devotions about God & Science*, *The Comeback*, *The Air I Breathe*, *I Am Not But I Know I Am*, and others. As a communicator, Louie is widely known for messages like Indescribable and How Great is Our God.

An Atlanta native and graduate of Georgia State University, Louie has done post-graduate work at Baylor University and holds a master's degree from Southwestern Baptist Theological Seminary. Louie and Shelley make their home in Atlanta.

Video Study for Your Church or Small Group

If you've enjoyed this book, now you can go deeper with the companion Bible study! In this six-session video study, Louie Giglio helps you apply the principles in *Seeing God as a Perfect Father* to your life. The study guide includes video notes, group discussion questions, and personal study materials for in between sessions.

Study Guide
with Streaming Video

DVD

Available now at your favorite bookstore
or streaming video on StudyGateway.com.

IT'S TIME TO WIN THE BATTLE OF YOUR MIND

The Jesus Bible

sixty-six books. one story. all about one name.

The Jesus Bible, NIV & ESV editions, with feature essays from Louie Giglio, Max Lucado, John Piper, and Randy Alcorn, as well as profound yet accessible study features will help you meet Jesus throughout Scripture.

- 350 full page articles
- 700 side-bar articles
- Book introductions
- Room for journaling

The Jesus Bible Journal, NIV
Study individual books of the Bible featuring lined journal space and commentary from *The Jesus Bible.*

- 14 journals covering 30 books of the Bible
- 2 boxed sets (OT & NT)

TheJesusBible.com